THE ULTIMATE
CHES
CYCLING GUIDE

EXCELLENT BOOKS

EXCELLENT BOOKS
94 BRADFORD ROAD
WAKEFIELD
WEST YORKSHIRE WF1 2AE
TEL / FAX: (01924) 315147

E-mail : richard@excellentbooks.co.uk
Website : www.excellentbooks.co.uk
Printed 2006

Text © Richard Peace 2005
Photographs and illustrations © Richard Peace

Street level mapping, unless otherwise stated, reproduced by permission of Philip's.
Licence no. 100011710
Maps in Cheshire Cycleway and Day Ride sections © Crown copyright 2005. All rights
reserved. Licence no. 100040135
All other maps based on OS mapping at least 50 years old at the time of compilation

ISBN 1 901464 19 9

Whilst the author has researched the routes for the purposes of this guide, r
responsibility can be accepted for any unforeseen circumstances encountered whil
following them. The publisher would, however, welcome any information regardir
any material changes and any problems encountered.

*Front cover photos (clockwise from top left): The Groves, Chester -
Cheshire Cycleway in Parkgate, the Wirral - A green lane near Cuddington -
Cheshire Cycleway above Bollington - Canal towpath in Chester
Rear cover photo: Bridge at Hockenhull Platts
Frontispiece: Middlewood Way near Higher Poynton*

The publishers would like to thank Cheshire County Council for all their help in th
compilation and publication of this book. They have also contributed heavily to th
implementation and maintenance of many of the routes described in it.

www.visit-cheshire.com

Contents

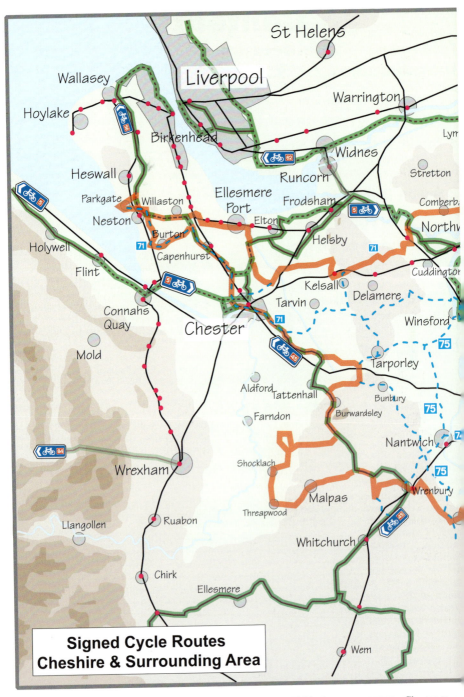

St Helens

Liverpool

Wallasey

Hoylake

Warrington

Birkenhead

Lym

Widnes

Stretton

Heswall

Ellesmere
Port

Runcorn

Frodsham

Comberb

Parkgate

Willaston

Elton

Helsby

Northw

Neston

Burton

Capenhurst

Cuddington

Holywell

71

71

Flint

Kelsall

Delamere

Connahs
Quay

Chester

Tarvin

Winsford

75

Mold

Tarporley

75

Aldford

Tattenhall

Bunbury

Farndon

Burwardsley

75

Nantwich

7

Shocklach

Wrexham

Malpas

Wrenbury

75

Llangollen

Ruabon

Threapwood

Whitchurch

45

Chirk

Ellesmere

Wem

**Signed Cycle Routes
Cheshire & Surrounding Area**

 Reading to
Holyhead

 Salisbury to
Chester

 Telford to
Preston

Chester to
Liverpool

4

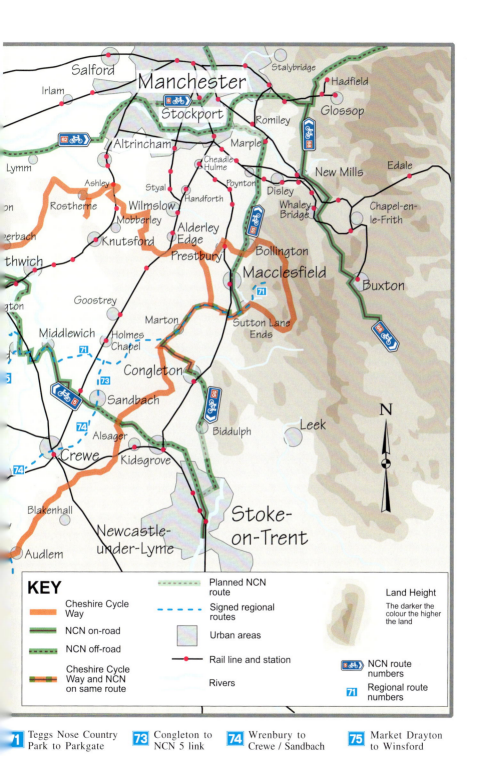

KEY

Cheshire Cycle Way (orange line)

NCN on-road (green line)

NCN off-road (green dashed line)

Cheshire Cycle Way and NCN on same route (orange and green line)

Planned NCN route (green dashed line)

Signed regional routes (blue dashed line)

Urban areas

Rail line and station

Rivers

Land Height
The darker the colour the higher the land

NCN route numbers

Regional route numbers

71 Teggs Nose Country Park to Parkgate

73 Congleton to NCN 5 link

74 Wrenbury to Crewe / Sandbach

75 Market Drayton to Winsford

Introduction

CYCLING IN CHESHIRE

Cheshire is undoubtedly a prosperous and beautiful county and it also happens to be a great place for cycling. Characterful towns and cities such as Chester, Macclesfield and Nantwich can all be cycled through easily and quickly leading you into some splendid countryside. Whether it's relaxing Sunday rides without traffic, longer day rides through the rolling heart of Cheshire or some of the most testing climbs in England you want, the county has it all. The best known traffic-free trails are locally well-known; Chester to Connah's Quay, the Whitegate Way and Delamere Forest hum with cyclists and walkers on a summer's weekend. This guide adds to these with perhaps less high profile but equally attractive trails such as the Wheelock Rail Trail and some lovely bridleways and byways. Link these together with quiet roads and you have a great selection of rides suitable for families or riders who prefer a leisurely pace and a comfortable distance.

Cheshire is famed for its half-timbered architecture ideally explored using the network of country lanes and tracks. Green, tree-lined pasture across much of the Cheshire Plain houses idyllic settlements which range from bustling market towns like Audlem, Malpas and Tarvin to tiny but unique village-cum-hamlets such as Peckforton. The overwhelmingly rural south-east corner provides some of the quietest riding but there is an abundance of attractive towns and villages across the county, from estate villages such as Rostherne to the unique estuarine setting of Parkgate on the Wirral peninsula. Good cycling opportunities pop up in the unlikeliest of places; ride across the marshes near the industrial hinterland of Ellesmere Port and you might see a peregrine falcon, whilst heading to nearby Frodsham offers the tough test of Overton Hill, with its remarkable views over the Weaver and Mersey towards Liverpool.

If you want truly testing riding amidst spectacular gritstone hill scenery there's no better place to head than the Cheshire Peak District. Gritstone edges are the outstanding features here, forming a complex series of valleys and ridges, some several kilometres long. Undoubtedly a test for even the fittest of cyclists, you'll find exhilarating riding with scenery to match the finest anywhere along the Pennine chain. The Cheshire Plain also has its own hill country, the Peckfortons. This sandstone ridge runs the length of Cheshire and gives some challenging riding and great views at a fraction of the effort needed to tackle Cheshire's Peak.

CHESHIRE CYCLEWAY & NATIONAL CYCLE NETWORK

The first five chapters of this book deal with the 176 mile, fully-signed touring route of the Cheshire Cycleway (chapters represent a suggested day's riding). A week would let you cycle the CCW at a reasonable pace; those not used to hills will want to avoid the steepest of the climbs by using the 'shortcut' via Henbury giving you a round trip of around 156 miles. The Cycleway was conceived by Bob Clift and implemented by Cheshire County Council who also do all the maintenance and signing.

The National Cycle Network (NCN) is the brainchild of cycling charity Sustrans. It criss-crosses Cheshire using a variety of minor roads, railpaths, canal towpaths and bridleways. It isn't simply for leisure use; its overriding concern is to provide safe, attractive well-signed routes to encourage cycling of all kinds. Sections of the NCN in Cheshire use many delightful sections of upgraded canal towpaths along the Trent and Mersey, Shropshire Union and Weaver navigations.

There are also regional routes; these may not be up to NCN standard but aim to provide handy links within the existing network (the Cheshire Cycleway is regional route 70). The day rides use a mixture of all these types of signed routes plus other roads and tracks. See the previous pages for all signed and numbered Cheshire cycle routes.

SIGNING EXPLAINED

National Cycle Network signs have a blue background and a red background to the appropriate route number. Regional Routes are coloured blue and white. Both come in a variety of formats and are usually posted at junctions, though you should always keep an eye out for smaller confirmatory signs, usually on poles supporting traffic signs. The Cheshire Cycleway is Regional Route 70 and is signed in both directions along its whole length. The Multi-day rides (pages 151-159) use sections of different numbered routes linked together, apart from Teggs Nose to Parkgate, which is route 71 along its entire length. Day rides and family rides may or may not use parts of NCN and Regional Routes. Some trails also have their own signs, for example the Bishop Bennet Trail is used in the Bishop's Trail day rides. Various types of NCN and Regional Route signs are explained below: (NB: Signs can go missing or get twisted - check your position against a good scale map if in doubt).

National Cycle Network route 45

Brackets indicate that the road or track leads to the numbered route

Regional Route 71

Some routes follow the same road or track - in this case Regional Routes 70 & 71

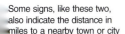

Some signs, like these two, also indicate the distance in miles to a nearby town or city

Follow the line of the arrow to NCN Route 45 and Regional Route 70

Unusually this sign shows the name of the trail that is straight ahead.

Keep your eyes peeled for the small confirmatory stickers as shown on the left. Millennium Mileposts are more rarely encountered and show distances to major settlements along the NCN as well as being an attractive design feature and providing a cryptic puzzle (more detail from Sustrans - see page 9). On the right is one on the Deeside Dawdle day ride.

THE CYCLISTS WELCOME SCHEME

Look out for this sign in hotels, B&Bs, pubs and cafes. If you see it you will know that the establishment displaying it has been contacted by Cheshire County Council and that they wish to actively encourage cyclists to visit them. This might mean anything from a cafe not minding the wet and muddy or could be a B&B with secure storage for cycles, packed lunches or route information. The first five chapters on the Cheshire Cycleway list what particular facilities accommodation providers have in detail (though not all of them participate in this scheme).

GETTING THERE AND AWAY

Cheshire is well-served for transport. There is a direct rail link into Manchester Airport, right on the northern border of the county, and the presence of Crewe in the county gives direct rail services to and from London and major regional cities such as Birmingham, Manchester, Liverpool, Edinburgh, Glasgow, Bristol and Cardiff. The northern sections of the Cheshire Cycleway and many of the day rides are well-served by local trains, operated by :

Central Trains - Tel 0121 634 2040 or see www.centraltrains.co.uk They operate the line from Birmingham through Winsford to Acton Bridge and Liverpool and the line from Derby into Alsager and through to Crewe.
Arriva Trains Wales operate lines from Manchester to Crewe and beyond, Manchester to Chester and beyond and Crewe to Nantwich and beyond. They can be contacted on 0845 6061 660 or see www.arrivatrainswales.co.uk
Virgin trains operate the Holyhead to Chester to Crewe line and the Warrington to Crewe line. They are on 08457 222 333 or www.virgin.com/trains
Northern Rail (0845 000 0125 – www.northernrail.org.uk) serve Ellesmere Port, running trains from Chester through stations on the northern sections of the Cheshire Cycleway and on to the north and serve Prestbury, Macclesfield and Congleton.
The "National Rail Guide - Cycling by train" is an excellent leaflet produced by Brompton Bicycle Ltd. and available at railway stations or downloadable from the national rail website (see opposite). It gives details of each company's rules for carrying bikes, always handy to have around when the area you're in has several train operating companies. Also worth considering is a bit of advance booking, especially if you're coming from some distance away – there are many cheap offers for travellers who are in a position to arrange things in advance.

Railway stations on or near the Cheshire Cycleway are: Chester, Capenhurst, Neston, Hooton, Little Sutton, Overpool, Ellesmere Port, Mouldsworth, Delamere, Cuddington, Acton Bridge, Ashley, Mobberley, Alderley Edge, Prestbury, Congleton, Alsager, Crewe, Wrenbury.

National Rail Enquiries : 08457 48 49 50   www.nationalrail.co.uk
Traveline : 0870 608 2608 or 01244 602666   www.traveline.org.uk
Transport Direct : www.transportdirect.info

FURTHER INFORMATION

Sustrans
National Cycle Network Centre.
2, Cathedral Square,
College Green
Bristol BS1 5DD
0845 113 0065
www.sustrans.org.uk

Byways Breaks
25, Mayville Road,
Liverpool L18 0HG
0151 722 8050
www.byways-breaks.co.uk

CTC
69, Meadrow,
Godalming
Surrey GU7 3HS
0870 873 0060
www.ctc.org.uk

YHA
Trevelyan House.
Dimple Road,
Matlock.
Derbyshire DE4 3YH
0870 7708868 / 01629 592600
www.yha.org.uk

Cheshire County Council
County Hall
Chester
Cheshire CH1 1SE
0845 11 333 11
www.cheshire.gov.uk

Websites
www.visit-cheshire.com
www.cheshire.gov.uk
www.peaksandplains.co.uk
www.cheshiredaysout.co.uk
www.cheshireforall.com
(access information for disabled people)

For cycling related matters you can also call Anna Geroni at Cheshire County Council direct on 01244 603617   Also see www.cheshire.gov.uk/cycling

KEY TO ACCOMMODATION ENTRY SYMBOLS

❶ B&Bs, hotels - cross reference to entries on Cheshire Cycleway maps
① Youth Hostels and campsites - cross reference to entries on Cheshire Cycleway maps
▭ Website address and / or e-mail address
£ Price for one person for one night sharing a twin or double room. Where breakfast is not included this is stated.
⌐ Number of rooms available and type: s=single t=twin d=double tr=triple f=family
♦♦/✷ ✷ Diamond / star ratings (previously AA, RAC and ETC ratings - now combined)
⦿ Meals available other than breakfast or nearby places to eat
⦿ Packed lunches with price and notice required
" Drying facilities
⌐ Laundry and price if applicable
⋈ Cycle storage
⚒ Tools available
⊟ Pick-up / drop-off service
⋏ Campsite with number of pitches if known and facilities as listed
⊥ Distance from route
Notes: "Open all year" does not normally include Christmas and New Year. Some of the accommodation entries will feature extra text after some of the above symbols giving extra information on the particular facilities. All entries correct at time of writing but subject to change; please check when booking to ensure facilities you require are available.

Great Peakland views on the Cheshire Cycleway above Bollington

9

CYCLING GROUPS IN CHESHIRE

If you're a resident of Cheshire there are lots of clubs to get involved in:
Chester Cycle Campaign Campaigns for better facilities and produces newsletters, family ride leaflets and more. See www.chestercycling.co.uk for more details
The following are road clubs and will be of interest to those who prefer organised road riding / road racing
Chester Road Club   Paul Evans 0151 339 2871
Chester & North Wales Cyclists Touring Club Martin Gooch 01829 740997 / Bob Turnbull 01244 344726
Congleton Cycling Group 01782 513972
Macclesfield Wheelers 01625 537401

Cycling for those with disabilities can be organised through the following:
New Scene Youth Centre (Newton Lane, Newton, Chester) have volunteered to supervise the use of 5 handbikes, a trike and a duet bike at the Youth Centre for use on the Millennium Cycle Route (Chester to Deeside - traffic free). In order to encourage families and friends to undertake this activity together, ordinary bikes have been provided to minimise the amount of equipment to be transported to the Youth Centre. Free of charge. For more information / to reserve a bike call 01244 320479.
Cycle Projects runs a scheme called Wheels for All which provides cycling opportunities for anyone who isn't able to manage a two-wheeled bike, for whatever reason. They have two bike hire centres in Cheshire - Alsager Leisure Complex (01270 875704) where you can use the cycles at a venue of your choice, and on the Wirral (Hadlow Road, Willaston Tel: 0151 327 5145) where you can use them along the Wirral Way, a disused railway line from Thurstaston to Parkgate. The Willaston centre also has cycles that can be used by family and friends. There is no longer a hire fee, but a donation towards the upkeep of the cycles and the purchasing of new equipment is encouraged. More information from 0161 745 9944.

CYCLE HIRE AND ORGANISED TRIPS

There are several cycle hire outlets in Cheshire:
Eureka Cycle Hire, Two Mills north of Chester 0151 3395629 Quality mountain bikes, hybrids and tandems. Delivery for a small charge within a 30 mile radius. From £8 per half day. All bikes with helmet, lock, spare tubes and repair kit. Group discount.
Tatton Park, near Knutsford 01827 284646
Wirraltracs, Delamere Forest 0151 3348098

Byways Breaks organise self-guided cycling (and walking) holidays in Cheshire as well as Shropshire and the Welsh Borders. You stay in one centre or tour the area staying at different overnight stops. Accommodation is in comfortable farms, country pubs, hotels or self-catering cottages. Offerings include tours from Chester and around the Peckfortons.

Contact Byways Breaks at 0151 7228050
info@byways-breaks.co.u
www.byways-breaks.co.uk

1 Chester - Acton Bridge

Route Info

45 miles / 72 km
Off - road 11 miles / 17.75 km
Height Ascended 473m / 1552ft

Using the excellent quality canal towpath of the
Shropshire Union out of Chester you then pick
up Sustrans National Cycle Network route 56
between Backford and Capenhurst, following
quiet lanes and specially made off-road paths.
There are dramatic views over the Dee
estuary's saltmarshes at Burton then a chance
to visit the famed Botanic Gardens at Ness. At
Parkgate you would once have seen the sea
but today you can look towards Wales across
miles of saltmarsh from its pretty 'seafront',
certainly one of the more unusual sights on the
cycleway. Pick up NCN 56 again in the form of
the off-road railpath, the Wirral Way, to pass
south of Willaston. Once through Ellesmere
Port you are back on the Shropshire Union
Canal. The Boat Museum here is a short and
worthwhile detour - even if you only go for the
impressive and unusual views over the Mersey
estuary towards Liverpool and Runcorn. A final
road section between Stoak and Acton Bridge
offers the lovely setting of Manley windsurfing
centre with its cafe, and the atmospheric
woods of Delamere Forest.

Looking from Burton towards Wales

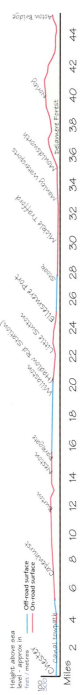

Chester Centre
suggested cycle routes

Cartography by Philip's © 2005 Philip's

© Crown copyright   Licence number 100011710

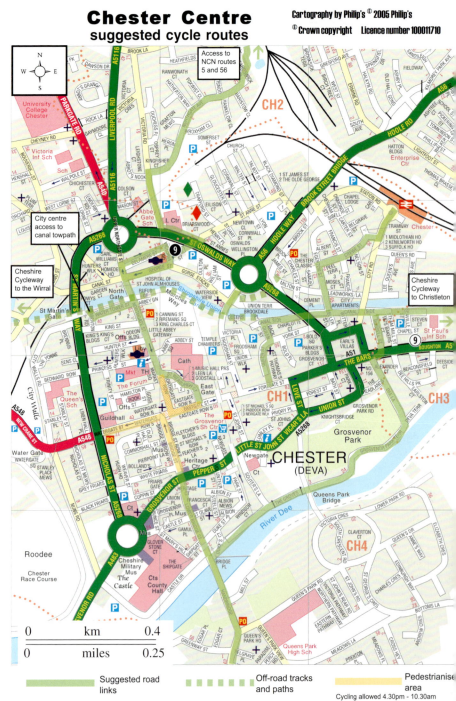

Access to NCN routes 5 and 56

City centre access to canal towpath

Cheshire Cycleway to the Wirral

Cheshire Cycleway to Christleton

Roodee

Chester Race Course

| 0 | km | 0.4 |
| 0 | miles | 0.25 |

Suggested road links

Off-road tracks and paths

Pedestrianised area
Cycling allowed 4.30pm - 10.30am

9 **9** Location of accommodation entries in Chapter 5 - see pages 62-63

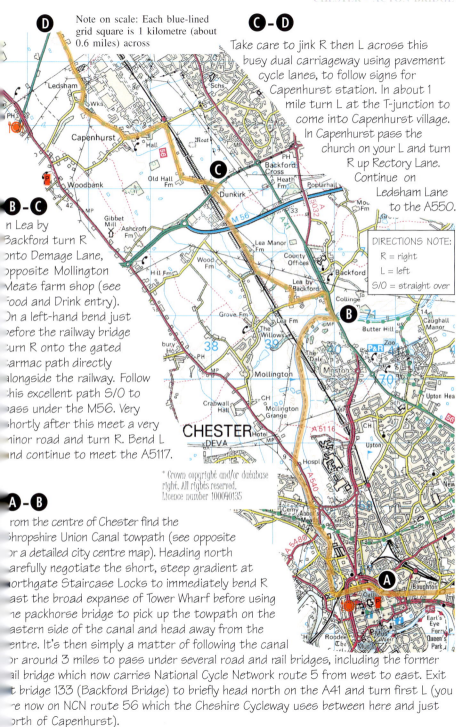

Note on scale: Each blue-lined grid square is 1 kilometre (about 0.6 miles) across

C - D

Take care to jink R then L across this busy dual carriageway using pavement cycle lanes, to follow signs for Capenhurst station. In about 1 mile turn L at the T-junction to come into Capenhurst village. In Capenhurst pass the church on your L and turn R up Rectory Lane. Continue on Ledsham Lane to the A550.

DIRECTIONS NOTE:
R = right
L = left
S/O = straight over

B - C

...n Lea by Backford turn R onto Demage Lane, opposite Mollington Meats farm shop (see Food and Drink entry). On a left-hand bend just before the railway bridge turn R onto the gated tarmac path directly alongside the railway. Follow this excellent path S/O to pass under the M56. Very shortly after this meet a very minor road and turn R. Bend L and continue to meet the A5117.

A - B

...rom the centre of Chester find the Shropshire Union Canal towpath (see opposite for a detailed city centre map). Heading north carefully negotiate the short, steep gradient at Northgate Staircase Locks to immediately bend R past the broad expanse of Tower Wharf before using the packhorse bridge to pick up the towpath on the eastern side of the canal and head away from the centre. It's then simply a matter of following the canal for around 3 miles to pass under several road and rail bridges, including the former rail bridge which now carries National Cycle Network route 5 from west to east. Exit at bridge 133 (Backford Bridge) to briefly head north on the A41 and turn first L (you are now on NCN route 56 which the Cheshire Cycleway uses between here and just north of Capenhurst).

© Crown copyright and/or database right. All rights reserved. Licence number 100040135

13

The route heads north out of Chester on well-surfaced towpath

Head along Parkgate front and turn R just before the Marsh Cat restaurant and immediate L at the split up School Lane. Bear L onto Brooklands Road. Pass the primary school to pick up the Wirral Way (NCN route 56), going under the little wooden bridge, bending L up the ramp on L onto the trail. On meeting the B road jink R then L to carry on, on the Wirral Way. Crossing over a bridge in Neston head S/O the car park area and under a rail bridge follow the road ahead, coming to T-junction with Mellock Lane / Bushell Rd at the end of Station Close . S/O here, back onto the traffic-free Wirral Way. Through the railway cutting continue on the obvious path of the Wirral Way,

past the restored station building. About 0.8 miles after the station come to a brick bridge over the trail and turn L off the trail (signed NCN route 56) to a road and R, to cross the bridge. Bend L, leaving NCN route 56, following signs for Childer Thornton. Follow to the end of Heath Lane and TAKE CARE crossing the A550.

See overleaf for route through Ellesmere Port.

ELLESMERE PORT

DIRECTIONS NOTE:
R = right
L = left
S/O = straight over

Note on scale: Each blue-lined grid square is 1 kilometre (about 0.6 miles) across

NESTON

© Crown copyright and/or database right. All rights reserved. Licence number 100040135

D – E

At the A550 head S/O using pavement cycle lanes. Turn L onto Badgers Rake Lane. Very shortly NCN Route 56 heads off R up a bridleway but you carry straight on to meet the A540. TAKE GREAT CARE to turn R and immediate L at the A540, following signs for Burton. In Burton the road swings R and uphill after passing through the village centre. Just here turn L and descend over the railway to fantastic views across the Dee estuary. Follow the road (Denhall Lane) as it bends 90 degrees R to climb to a T-junction. Turn L to come to Ness Botanic Gardens. Just before the Wheatsheaf pub turn L onto Well Lane. There are more views over the Dee from here before meeting the road in Neston and going L. S/O a mini-roundabout, following Burton Road into Neston, head S/O across a roundabout and in Neston bear L by the drinking fountain onto The Cross, becoming Parkgate Road. Follow this road all the way into Parkgate and head along the 'front' with spectacular marsh views.

15

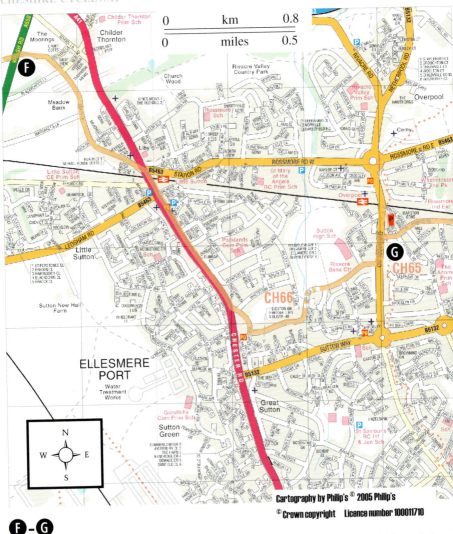

Cartography by Philip's © 2005 Philip's
© Crown copyright   Licence number 100011710

F - G

Follow the road through Childer Thornton. At the A41 turn R onto the roadside cycle lane and follow this for about 0.6 miles, into Great Sutton, before turning L onto Old Chester Road. Turn L by the White Swan pub onto Mill Lane, continuing on at the end, onto a tarmac path by a brook on the L. The path rejoins Mill Lane and continues to the main road (Overpool Rd). Turn L and immediate R at the traffic lights onto Princes Road, just before the Wheatsheaf pub.

G - H

Head through the estate to meet the A5032 and go S/O onto Cromwell Road (Ellesmere Port train station is to the L here). Continue on Cromwell Road until you meet the canal. Heading L onto the towpath means you can visit the Boat Museum in 0.5 miles, where the canal meets the Manchester Ship Canal, whilst the Cheshire Cycleway goes R on the towpath. Heading south on the towpath immediately pass under the M53.

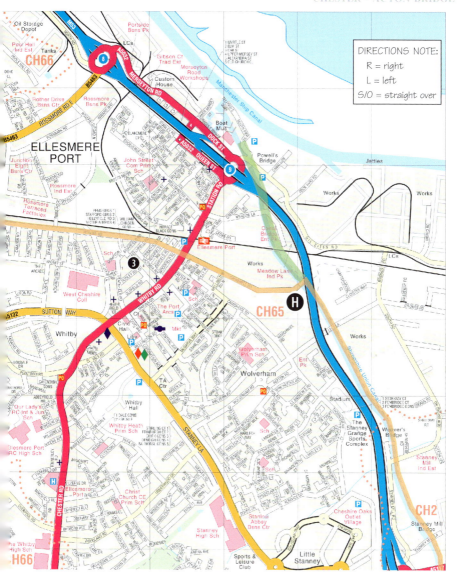

Optional 'there and back' detour along the towpath to
Ellesmere Port Boat Museum

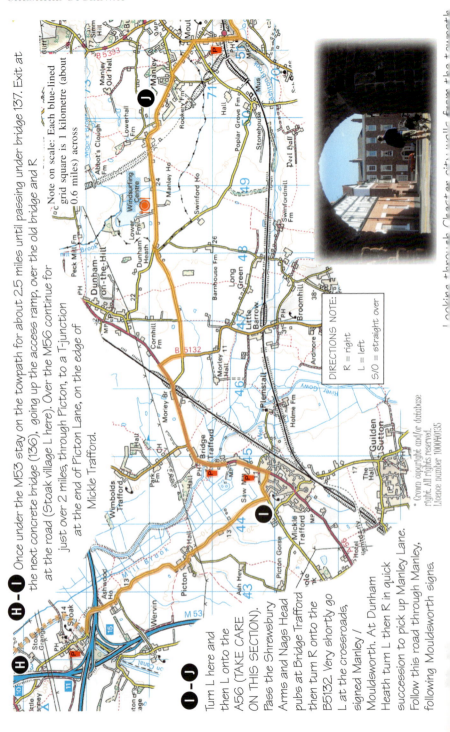

H–I

Once under the M53 stay on the towpath for about 2.5 miles until passing under bridge 137. Exit at the next concrete bridge (136), going up the access ramp, over the old bridge and R at the road (Stoak village L here). Over the M56 continue for just over 2 miles, through Picton, to a T-junction at the end of Picton Lane, on the edge of Mickle Trafford.

Note on scale: Each blue-lined grid square is 1 kilometre (about 0.6 miles) across

DIRECTIONS NOTE:

R = right

L = left

S/O = straight over

I–J

Turn L here and then L onto the A56 (TAKE CARE ON THIS SECTION). Pass the Shrewsbury Arms and Nags Head pubs at Bridge Trafford then turn R onto the B5132. Very shortly go L at the crossroads, signed Manley / Mouldsworth. At Dunham Heath turn L then R in quick succession to pick up Manley Lane. Follow this road through Manley, following Mouldsworth signs.

Looking through Chester city walls from the towpath

© Crown copyright and/or database right. All rights reserved. Licence number 100040135

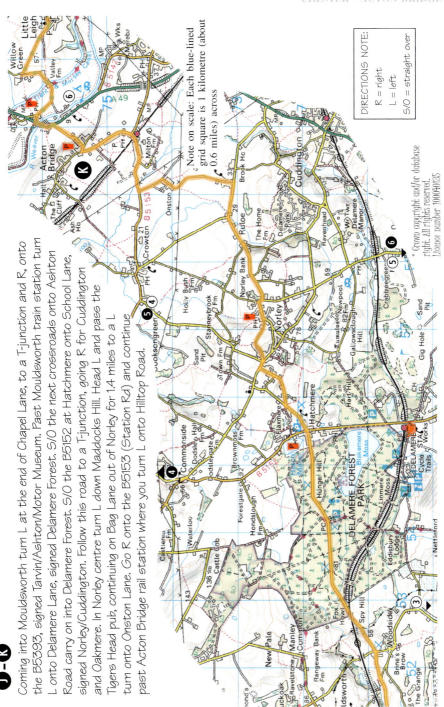

* Crown copyright and/or database right. All rights reserved. Licence number 100040135

DIRECTIONS NOTE:

R = right

L = left

S/O = straight over

Note on scale: Each blue-lined grid square is 1 kilometre (about 0.6 miles) across

J - K

Coming into Mouldsworth turn L at the end of Chapel Lane, to a T-junction and R, onto the B5393, signed Tarvin/Ashton/Motor Museum. Past Mouldsworth train station turn L onto Delamere Lane, signed Delamere Forest. S/O the next crossroads onto Ashton Road carry on into Delamere Forest. S/O the B5152 at Hatchmere onto School Lane, signed Norley/Cuddington. Follow this road to a T-junction, going R for Cuddington and Oakmere. In Norley centre turn L down Maddocks Hill. Head L and pass the Tigers Head pub, continuing on Bag Lane out of Norley for 1.4 miles to a L turn onto Onston Lane. Go R onto the B5153 (Station Rd) and continue past Acton Bridge rail station where you turn L onto Hilltop Road.

19

Hotels and Guesthouses

CHESTER TO ACTON BRIDGE

❶ TUDOR ROSE PREMIER TRAVEL INN   2 Mills   Wirral CH66 9PD (0151 339 2399)
£49.95 per room per night Monday - Thursday, £46.95 Friday to Sunday   31 rooms
Tourist Information Centre listed   breakfast £5.25 for Lighter Bite or £6.95 for full English
Fully licensed restaurant   flasks and bottle-filling   laundry service on request
    Open all year   1 mile

❷ THE SHIP The Parade Parkgate Wirral CH64 6SA (0151 336 3931)
www.the-shiphotel.co.uk   £60.00 per double or twin room per night including continental
breakfast   2 four poster 2 triple 4t 7d 9s   Tourist Information Centre listed
lunch available   £3.00   laundrette close by   Pressure hose for bike washing
Open all year including Christmas and New Year   on the route

❸ HEATH LODGE   87 - 89 Heathfield Road Ellesmere Port CH65 8DH (0151 357 2246)
£22.00 during the week £25.00 weekends   4t   Tea and coffee in rooms Shared
bathrooms   Jet wash and hose for bike washing Only closed on Christmas Day and
New Year's Day   near route

❹ CHARNWOOD BED & BREAKFAST Hollow Lane Kingsley Nr. Frodsham WA6 8EF
(01928 787097)   www.smoothhound.co.uk/hotels/charnwood   From £20.00 to £27.50
    1d1t Tourist Information Centre listed   10% discount off food at pub 2 minutes walk
away   Always open   2 miles

❺ THE POPLARS   Norley Lane Crowton Northwich CW8 2RR (01928 788083)
www.the-poplarsbandb.co.uk   £30.00   1t2d all en suite   ♦♦♦♦   Tourist Information
Centre listed   excellent pub within half a mile   Flask and bottle filling with notice
radiators and electric heaters in rooms throughout the year   Hose available for bike
washing   Open all year   0.8 miles

❻ ELM COTTAGE CARAVAN PARK AND BED AND BREAKFAST Chester Lane Little
Budworth Winsford CW7 2QJ (01829 760544)   www.elmcottagecp.co.uk   £20.00 - £30.00
    2d/t1f ♦♦♦   Tourist Information Centre listed   48hours notice   tumble dryer, radiators
    washing machine and tumble dryer   Compressed air line and basic tools available
Open all year except Christmas and New Year and 1st - 14th February   5 miles

The old Willaston station on the Wirral Way

An attractive canalside route into Chester centre

Hostels and Campsites

CHESTER TO ACTON BRIDGE

① RABY PARK PADDOCK Raby Park Road Neston CH64 9FX (07956 534035) **A** Toilets and showers (including toilet accessible to disabled people) Open all year Ring in advance to arrange Good shops, restaurants and pubs in nearby Neston 🚲 0.8 miles

② CHESTER FAIROAKS CARAVAN SITE Rake Lane Little Stanney CH2 4HS (01513 551600) **A** Toilets Showers ⬚ Open to tents mid-April to mid-September Plenty of places to eat locally 🚲 about 1 mile

③ NORTHWOOD HALL COUNTRY TOURING PARK Dog Lane Kelsall CW6 0RP (01829 752569) 🖥 www.northwood-hall.co.uk **A** Toilets and showers Open 1st March to 31st October 🚲 about 2 miles

④ THE POPLARS Norley Lane Crowton Northwich CW8 2RR (01928 788083) 🖥 www.the-poplarsbandb.co.uk **A** two and a half acre campsite and five caravan pitches 🚲 0.8 miles

⑤ ELM COTTAGE CARAVAN PARK AND BED AND BREAKFAST Chester Lane Little Budworth Winsford CW7 2QJ (01829 760544) 🖥 www.elmcottagecp.co.uk **A** 25 ✱ ✱ ✱ £8.25 - £10.50 per pitch includes 2 adults and 2 children 🍴 48 hours notice ⌐ ⬚ 🚲 Compressed air line and basic tools available Open all year except 1st - 14th February 🚲 5 miles

⑥ WOODBINE COTTAGE CARAVAN PARK Warrington Road Acton Bridge CW8 3QB (01606 852319) **A** Toilets Showers ⬚ washing up sinks On the banks of the River Weaver Next to Riverside Inn which does food every day Open 1st March to 31st October 🚲 about a quarter of a mile

21

Food and Drink Suggestions

Note: The listings below are not comprehensive.
See red symbols on maps for the location of even more cafes (🍽) and pubs (P)

MOLLINGTON MEATS Friars Park Farm Mollington (01244 851333) A farm butchers with local meat also selling cakes, soft fruit and vegetables as well as ice cream. 🏃 On the route

EUREKA CYCLISTS CAFE Parkgate Road Woodbank Chester CH1 6EZ (0151 339 5629) 💻 www.eurekacyclistscafe.co.uk Breakfasts, sandwiches, traditional English snacks, homemade cakes, speciality coffees, herbal teas Open Wednesday 8.30 - 5.00, Friday 10.00 - 4.00, Saturday and Sunday 8.30 - 5.00 and Bank Holidays 9.00 - 4.00 Closed at Christmas Also offer a full range of cycle accessories from the cafe or by mail order, cycle route information and leaflets and cycle hire 🚲 🏃 one mile

THE HARP INN 19 Quayside Little Neston CH64 0TB (0151 336 6980) 💻 www.harpinn.co.uk   Cask ale pub alongside the route on the marsh front at Little Neston. Little Neston is a site of scientific interest, an RSPB reserve and of historic interest   See website for range of beers 🏃 0.6 miles

THE COACH & HORSES 11 Bridge Street Neston CH64 9UH (0151 336 5335) 💻 jacqueline_grobbelar@yahoo.co.uk Basic burgers and chips through to Sunday lunch and speciality dishes from South Africa   Food available 12.00 - 7.00 £5.00 - £10.00 🏃 100 metres

THE LODESTAR 20 - 24 Brooke Street Neston CH64 9XL (0151 336 0233) Full range of hot and cold snacks and meals from under £5.00 up to £10.00 Food available 11.00 - 10.00 🚲 🏃 near the route

PARKGATE COFFEE SHOP The Parade Parkgate CH64 6SB (0151 336 4414) Snacks, full meals, sandwiches, toasties, baked potato Start at £2.00 and go up to £6.00 Open Tuesday to Friday 9.30 - 4.30/5.00 and Saturday and Sunday 10.00 - 4.30 Closed Monday Open all year except Christmas period and annual holidays 🏃 on route

THE NAGS HEAD Hooton Road Willaston Wirral CH64 1SJ (0151 237 2439) Home-cooked English meals from under £5.00 up to £10.00 available 12.00 - 7.30 (6.30 on Sunday) Fully stocked bar with three guest ales Cycle club meets at the Nags on a Tuesday 🚲 🏃 quarter of a mile

THE HOOTON HOTEL Hooton Road Hooton Ellesmere Port CH66 7NL 💻 info@hootonhotel.co.uk   (0151 327 2750)   Open all day every day   English food Price range for full meal and drink £5.00 - £10.00   🏃 0.5 miles (continue to end of Wirral Way)

THE CHESHIRE YEOMAN Ledsham Road Little Sutton CH66 4QR (0151 339 3106) 💻 ches-yeo@tiscali.co.uk Traditional English and foreign food Full meals, specials, vegetarian and bar snacks Prices up to £10.00 Available 12.00 - 8.30 Monday to Thursday, 12.00 - 9.00 Friday and Saturday and 12.00 - 8.00 Sunday 🏃 0.5 miles

WHITE SWAN Old Chester Road Great Sutton Ellesmere Port Food lunchtimes and evenings Mon-Sat. 1pm-7pm Sun. 🏃 On the route

SAIL SPORTS Manley Mere Manley Lane Manley WA6 0PE (01928 740243) Manley Mere is a sailing and windsurfing centre which also has an adventure trail. The bar/cafe is overlooking the lake and serves delicious capuccino, homemade cakes and traditional English snacks Meal and drink under £5.00 Open 10.00 - 6.00 every day from March to 31st October and on Saturdays and Sundays only from November to March 🚲 🏃 0.2 of a mile

THE MAYPOLE INN 59 Hill Top Road Acton Bridge CW8 3RA (01606 853114) Snacks from £5.00, main meals from £7.95   Open Monday to Saturday 11.30 - 3.00 (food 12.00 - 2.00) and evenings (food 6.00 - 9.30)   Sunday 12.00 - 3.30 and 6.00 - 10.30 (food 12.00 - 2.30 and 6.00 - 9.30) 🚲 🏃 on route

HAZEL PEAR INN Acton Bridge Opposite the railway station (01606 853195) Food lunchtime and evenings 🏃 on the route

Visitor Attractions

CHESTER ZOO Upton by Chester CH2 1LH (01244 380280) 🖥 www.chesterzoo.org Ring or see website for hours and charges which change according to time of year 🚲about 1 mile

DEE ESTUARY SALTFLATS Unusually, used for wildfowling and as a military firing range. 🚲On the route just after BURTON, a picturesque village with timber-framed cottages.

NESS BOTANIC GARDENS Cafe, gift shop and plant sales. Admission charge to gardens. Open daily 🚲On the route just after Burton

NESTON is a pleasant, busy little town - market day Friday - and PARKGATE, right on the north west corner of the Cheshire Cycleway, is a one-time port which owing to silting now enjoys panoramic marshland views with the hills of Wales as a memorable backdrop. The promenade has cafes and ice cream parlours and all the feel of the seaside

WILLASTON, by the Wirral Country Park, has shops, a post office, a village green, a windmill and some fine timbered buildings. Hadlow Road station on the Cycleway is now a museum showing how the station would have been in 1952 when it was closed

ELLESMERE PORT attractions include THE BOAT MUSEUM and BLUE PLANET AQUARIUM - see below for details Other attractions range from large shopping complexes to a good number of country parks and the area around the boat museum has interesting views of the Manchester Ship Canal and across the estuary to Liverpool

THE BOAT MUSEUM South Pier Road Ellesmere Port CH65 4FW 🖥www.boatmuseum.org.uk Open 10.00 - 5.00 every day April to October(inc) and 11.00 - 4.00 Saturday to Wednesday November to March (inc) Seven acre industrial heritage site with exhibitions in original dock buildings including interactive displays, cafe and shop, period cottages, traditional boats. Boat trip available, events throughout the year,children's workshops in school holidays.Toilets in entrance Cafe accessible on entry offering traditional English snacks, Costa coffee, salads, panini etc. Picnic tables available   🚲0.5 miles

BLUE PLANET AQUARIUM Cheshire Oaks Ellesmere Port CH65 9LF (0151 357 8800) 🖥 www.blueplanetaquarium.co.uk Huge aquarium including underwater moving walkway to view sharks and other fish Admission charge 🚲about 1 mile

MANLEY MERE SAIL SPORTS WINDSURFING CENTRE (01928 740243) Cafe & toilets See Food and Drink section for details

MOULDSWORTH MOTOR MUSEUM Smithy Lane Mouldsworth CH3 8AR (01928 731781) 🖥 www.mouldsworthmotormuseum.com Cars, motorcycles and early bicycles Open Sunday afternoons and all Bank Holiday weekends February until the end of November, also Wednesdays in July and August   Admission charge   🚲about 500yards

DELAMERE FOREST PARK VISITOR CENTRE Linmere Delamere CW8 2JD (01606 889792) 🖥 www.forestry.gov.uk/northwestengland   Cafe serving sandwiches, hot food, hot and cold drinks and snacks   Visitor centre   Shop   Information on forest cycle routes   Adjacent bike hire (Wirraltracs) and bikewash   Picnic tables   Open every day except Christmas Day - 10.00 - 5.00 April to September and 10.00 - 4.00 October to March   Cycle parking facility, although not secure 🚲one mile

NORLEY has the Tiger's Head pub and a nice little general shop in Pytchleys Hollow on the route as you pass the village

ACTON BRIDGE is a small village near the River Weaver Nearby is the Woodland Trust's Hazel Pear Wood and the road bridge over the Weaver is very photogenic Cluster of pubs, with food, in the area

Bike Shops

Eureka Cyclists Cafe See page 22 for full contact and other details. Stocks cycle accessories, route information and leaflets and does cycle hire.
W Homer Cycles 7-9 Enfield Road Ellesmere Port CH65 8DA 0151 3552130
🖳www.whomercycles.co.uk   🚲200yards
Big Bills Bikes Unit 48 Ellesmere Port Market Ellesmere Port CH65 0AP 0151 3551100
🖳www.bigbillsbikes.co.uk   🚲200yards

Tourist Information

Ellesmere Port Tourist Information Centre
Unit 22b Cheshire Oaks Outlet Village Kinsey Road Ellesmere Port CH65 9JJ
(0151 356 7879)   🖳www.cheshireoakstic.com   🖳www.visitchester.com

Attractive architecture along Parkgate's 'seafront'

2 Acton Bridge - Bollington

Route Info

Acton Bridge - Bollington
35 miles / 56 km   Off - road 0 miles / 0 km
Height Ascended 506m / 1661ft
Acton Bridge to Warren
34 miles / 54km   Off - road 0 miles / 0 km
Height Ascended 470m / 1541ft
Using the 'Henbury' shortcut reduces the
overall length of the Cheshire Cycleway
from 176 miles to 156 miles.

Although even minor roads can be busy
at rush hour round here (many villages
are Manchester 'dormitory' settlements)
there is much to enjoy, especially if you
can avoid peak traffic times when the
roads can be much quieter. Initially the
landscape is pleasant and agricultural,
but after passing north of Nether
Alderley it changes as you start to climb
towards the Peak District. Wooded
hillsides dip and roll and the gradients are
short but noticeably sharper than anything
that has come before.
For an easier option, avoiding most of
section 3, with its very steep Pennine
gradients, you can head south on the
signed 'Henbury Loop', leaving the
harder option about halfway between
NetherAlderley and Prestbury. No need
to feel you've wimped out if you take
this option; section 3 is a real challenge
even for the fittest of riders, so a
minimum level of reasonable fitness is
the very least you want if heading on to
Bollington and beyond.

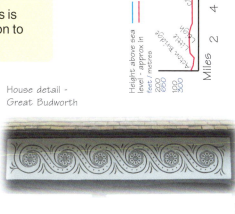

Bollington

Prestbury

Turning for Henbury Loop
(See profile below, rest of loop)

Ashley

Rossmere
(Acton Hall)

Buxklow Hill

High Legh

Great Budworth

Comberbach

Little
Leigh

Acton Bridge

Height above sea
level - approx in
feet / metres

Off-road surface
On-road surface

Miles

Height above sea
level - approx in
feet / metres

Off-road surface
On-road surface

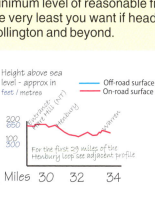

Entrance -
Marple Hill (NT)

Henbury

Warren

200
650

100
300

For the first 29 miles of the
Henbury loop see adjacent profile

Miles 30   32   34

House detail -
Great Budworth

25

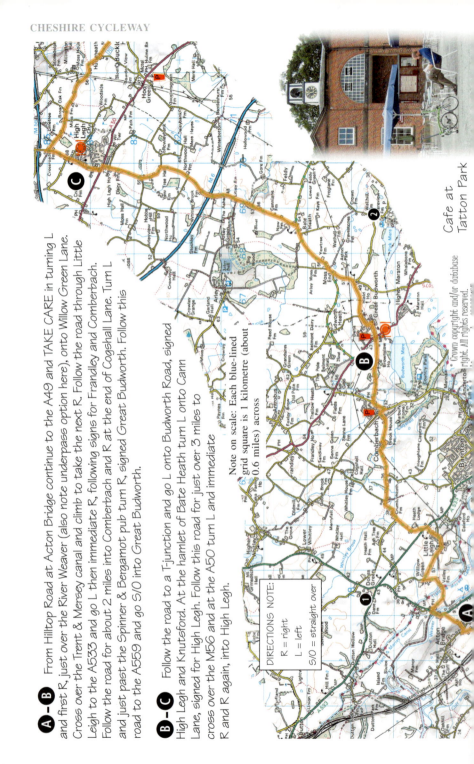

Cafe at Tatton Park

Crown copyright and/or database right. All rights reserved.

A – B From Hilltop Road at Acton Bridge continue to the A49 and TAKE CARE in turning L and first R, just over the River Weaver (also note underpass option here), onto Willow Green Lane. Cross over the Trent & Mersey canal and climb to take the next R. Follow the road through Little Leigh to the A533 and go L then immediate R, following signs for Frandley and Comberbach. Follow the road for about 2 miles into Comberbach and R at the end of Cogshall Lane. Turn L and just past the Spinner & Bergamot pub turn R, signed Great Budworth. Follow this road to the A559 and go S/O into Great Budworth.

B – C Follow the road to a T junction and go L onto Budworth Road, signed High Legh and Knutsford. At the hamlet of Bate Heath turn L onto Cann Lane, signed for High Legh. Follow this road for just over 3 miles to cross over the M56 and at the A50 turn L and immediate R and R again, into High Legh.

Note on scale: Each blue-lined grid square is 1 kilometre (about 0.6 miles) across

DIRECTIONS NOTE:
R = right
L = left
S/O = straight over

26

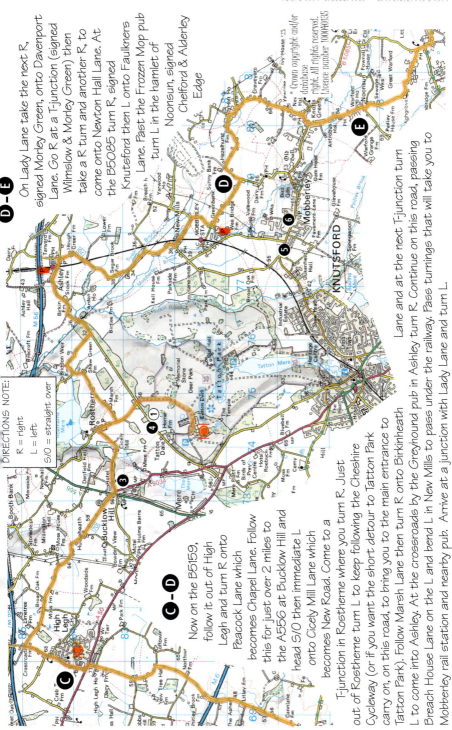

D – E

On Lady Lane take the next R, signed Morley Green, onto Davenport Lane. Go R at a T-junction (signed Wilmslow & Morley Green) then take a R turn and another R, to come onto Newton Hall Lane. At the B5085 turn R, signed Knutsford then L onto Faulkners Lane. Past the Frozen Mop pub turn L in the hamlet of Noonsun, signed Chelford & Alderley Edge

© Crown copyright and/or database right. All rights reserved. Licence number 100040135

DIRECTIONS NOTE:

R = right
L = left
S/O = straight over

C – D

Now on the B5159, follow it out of High Legh and turn R onto Peacock Lane which becomes Chapel Lane. Follow this for just over 2 miles to the A556 at Bucklow Hill and head S/O then immediate L onto Cicely Mill Lane which becomes New Road. Come to a T-junction in Rostherne where you turn R. Just out of Rostherne turn L to keep following the Cheshire Cycleway (or if you want the short detour to Tatton Park carry on, on this road, to bring you to the main entrance to Tatton Park). Follow Marsh Lane then turn R onto Birkinheath L to come into Ashley. At the crossroads by the Greyhound pub in Ashley turn R. Continue on this road, passing Breach House Lane on the L and bend L in New Mills to pass under the railway. Pass turnings that will take you to Mobberley rail station and nearby pub. Arrive at a junction with Lady Lane and turn L. Lane and at the next T-junction turn

27

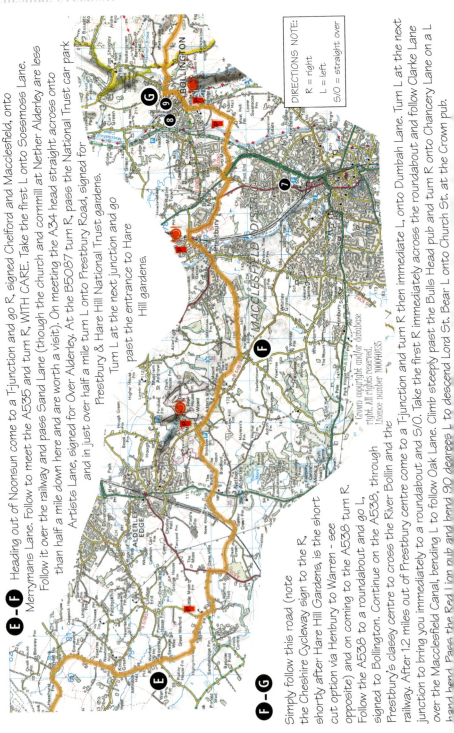

DIRECTIONS NOTE:

R = right

L = left

S/O = straight over

E – F Heading out of Noonsun come to a T-junction and go R, signed Chelford and Macclesfield, onto Merrymans Lane. Follow to meet the A535 and turn R, WITH CARE. Take the first L onto Sossomas Lane. Follow it over the railway and pass Sand Lane (though the church and cornmill at Nether Alderley are less than half a mile down here and are worth a visit). On meeting the A34 head straight across onto Artists Lane, signed for Over Alderley. At the B5087 turn R, pass the National Trust car park and in just over half a mile turn L onto Prestbury Road, signed for Prestbury & Hare Hill National Trust gardens.

Turn L at the next junction and go past the entrance to Hare Hill gardens.

F – G Simply follow this road (note the Cheshire Cycleway sign to the R, shortly after Hare Hill Gardens, is the short cut option via Henbury to Warren – see opposite) and on coming to the A538 turn R.

Follow the A538 to a roundabout and go L, signed to Bollington. Continue on the A538, through Prestbury's classy centre to cross the River Bollin and the railway. After 1.2 miles out of Prestbury centre come to a T-junction and turn R then immediate L, onto Dumbah Lane. Turn L at the next junction to bring you immediately to a roundabout and S/O. Take the first R immediately across the roundabout and follow Clarke Lane over the Macclesfield Canal, bending L to follow Oak Lane. Climb steeply past the Bulls Head pub and turn R onto Chancery Lane on a L hand bend. Pass the Red Lion pub and bend 90 degrees L to descend Lord St. Bear L onto Church St. at the Crown pub.

Crown copyright and/or database right. All rights reserved. Licence number 100040135

DIRECTIONS FOR SHORTER ROUTE OPTION VIA HENBURY TO WARREN

(A) - (B) Shortly after passing Hare Hill Gardens entrance look out for the R signed for Chelford and shortly meet the B5087 and head R then L. Take the next L signed Henbury and Broken Cross. At the end of Wrigley Lane go L onto Whirley Lane and next R onto Andertons Lane. Continue into Henbury, turning R off Church Lane onto Pepper Street. Head straight across the A537 onto School Lane.

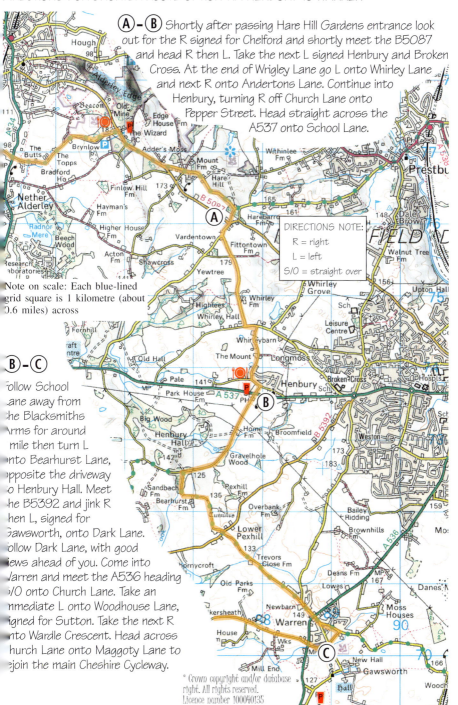

DIRECTIONS NOTE:

R = right

L = left

S/O = straight over

Note on scale: Each blue-lined grid square is 1 kilometre (about 0.6 miles) across

(B) - (C)

Follow School Lane away from the Blacksmiths Arms for around a mile then turn L onto Bearhurst Lane, opposite the driveway to Henbury Hall. Meet the B5392 and jink R then L, signed for Gawsworth, onto Dark Lane. Follow Dark Lane, with good views ahead of you. Come into Warren and meet the A536 heading S/O onto Church Lane. Take an immediate L onto Woodhouse Lane, signed for Sutton. Take the next R onto Wardle Crescent. Head across Church Lane onto Maggoty Lane to rejoin the main Cheshire Cycleway.

° Crown copyright and/or database right. All rights reserved. Licence number 100040135

29

Villages don't get much more picturesque than Great Budworth

Hotels and Guesthouses

ACTON BRIDGE TO BOLLINGTON

❶ TALL TREES LODGE Tarporley Road Lower Whitley WA4 4EZ (01928 790824) 🖥 www.talltreeslodge.co.uk £42.50 per room per night including continental breakfast 🚲 20t&f ✦✦✦ Tourist Information Centre listed ⊺ ⊡ 🚲 Open all year 🚶0.8 miles

❷ PICKMERE COUNTRY GUEST HOUSE Park Lane Pickmere Knutsford WA16 0JX (01565 733433) 🖥 www.pickmerehouse.co.uk £30.00 🚲 1s1t5d4f ✦✦✦ Tourist Information Centre listed 🍴£5.00 24hours notice ⊺drying room and c/h radiators ⊡ 🔧 🚲 Open all year 🚶two miles

❸ PREMIER TRAVEL INN Bucklow Hill WA16 6RD (0870 9906428) On the route

❹ TATTONDALE FARM Tatton Park Ashley Road Knutsford WA16 6QJ (01565 654692) 🖥 tattondalefarm@bigfoot.com £20.00 - £22.50 🚲 1s1t1d ⊺and⊡available by arrangement 🔧basic tools 🚲 Situated inside National Trust Park TV and tea and coffee-making facilities in rooms Transport needed for nearest pub/town/eateries Open all year 🚶about one mile

❺ LABURNUM COTTAGE Knutsford Road Mobberley WA16 7PU (01565 872464) £28.50 🚲 2t1d2s ✦✦✦✦ Tourist Information Centre listed 🍴three course dinner with wine £15.00 🍴 charge dependent ⊺ ⊡ 🚲 Open all year - 🚶about 1 mile

❻ THE HINTON Town Lane Mobberley WA16 7HH (01565 873484) 🖥 the.hinton@virgin.com £29.00 🚲 2d2s1f ✦✦✦✦ Tourist Information Centre listed 🍴 three course meal by arrangement £15.00 🍴£5.00 - notice previous evening ⊺drying room and tumble dryer ⊡ Open all year including Christmas and New Year 🚶0.7 miles

❼ MOORHAYES HOUSE 27 Manchester Road Tytherington Macclesfield SK10 2JJ (01625 433228) 🖥 www.smoothhound.co.uk £30.00 🚲 2f4d1t1s ✦✦✦ Tourist Information Centre listed 🍴£5.00 - no charge for flask-filling ⊺communal drying room available ⊡ laundrette 3 minutes walk away 🚲 Open all year except Christmas and New Year 🚶half a mile

❽ RED OAKS FARM Charter Road Bollington Macclesfield SK10 5NU (01625 574280) 🖥 bb@redoaks.go-plus.net £27.50 - £30.00 🚲 1d2t ✦✦✦✦ Tourist Information Centre listed 🍴 two course evening meal from £12.50 🍴 from £4.50 - notice on arrival ⊺ ⊡ 🚲 Open all year 🚶route passes along Jackson Lane which is 400 yards from the farmhouse

❾ HOLLIN HALL HOTEL Jackson Lane Bollington SK10 5BG (01625 573246) 🖥 www.hollinhallhotel.com £25.00 - £35.00 🚲 15t 3s 40d ★★★ Tourist Information Centre listed 🍴table d'hote set dinner £19.50 🍴£5.00 ⊺ ⊡ 🚲 Open all year 🚶500yards

Tatton Mere, Tatton Park

Hostels and Campsites

ACTON BRIDGE TO BOLLINGTON

① TATTONDALE FARM Tatton Park Ashley Road Knutsford WA16 6QJ (01565 654692)
📧tattondalefarm@bigfoot.com ▲phone for details 🚲about one mile

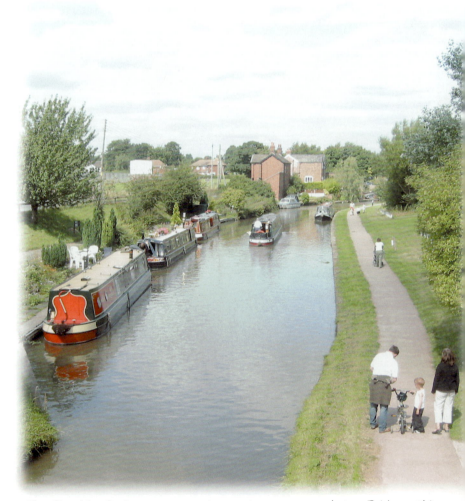

The Cheshire Cycleway crosses two waterways near Acton Bridge - this
one is the Trent & Mersey

The Leigh Arms sits between the River Weaver and the Trent & Mersey Canal

Food and Drink Suggestions

Note: The listings below are not comprehensive.
See red symbols on maps for the location of even more cafes (🍽) and pubs (🅿)

GREAT BUDWORTH REAL DAIRY ICE CREAM New Westage Farm Great Budworth CW9 6ND (01606 891211)   💻 www.icecreamfarm.co.uk   Light lunches, soup, sandwiches, toasties, home-made cakes and scones   Open daily 12.00 - 6.00 1st April to 31st October with lunches served weekdays 12.00 - 2.00   Under £5.00 for full meal and drink   Open weekends only 1.00 - 5.00 during November, December and March   🚲   Great Budworth is a beautiful village and has always been a welcome stop for cyclists The tearoom has some very old postcards of cyclists in Great Budworth 🚴 200 yards

THE WIZARD TEAROOM Macclesfield Road Nether Alderley SK10 4UB (01625 572706) 💻 wendy.scott@uku.co.uk Popular weekend tearoom at a National Trust wooded walking area Used by cyclists and always happy to see more Large NT car park and smaller tearoom car park Plenty of posts and rail fencing to lock bikes to   Breakfasts, snacks, light meals, cakes, scones (all homemade) Tea, coffee,soft drinks Full meal and drink from under £5.00 Open Saturday, Sunday and Bank Holidays 10.00 - 5.00 Closed Christmas Day and Boxing Day Will open by arrangement during the week for parties of 15+   🚴 on the route

THE LORD CLYDE 36 Clarke Lane Kerridge SK10 5AH (01625 562123) 💻 thelordclyde@btconnect.com   snacks and full meals, a la carte in the evenings Price range for full meal and drink £5.00 - £10.00 Open 12.00 - 11.00 with food available 12.00 - 3.00 and 7.00 - 10.00 Monday to Saturday and 12.00 - 9.00 on Sunday   Bangers and Jazz on a Tuesday evening 🚴 on the route

There are plenty of cafes, pubs and restaurants in Alderley Edge and Prestbury, though if you are looking for budget options it's better to wait until BOLLINGTON which boasts the excellent value sandwich shops and bakeries on its main shopping street, Palmerston St (B5090) and a variety of pubs.

HENBURY SHORTCUT:
AJ'S AND FLORA TEAROOM Flora Garden Centre Chelford Road Henbury Macclesfield SK11 9PG (01625 502300)   Open 9.00 - 5.00 Tuesday to Saturday and 10.00 - 5.00 on Sunday Closed Monday   Range of starters and main courses with sweet counter and snack menu Price range for full meal and drink £5.00 - £10.00   🚴 on the route
Also in Henbury is the BLACKSMITH'S ARMS, a Chef and Brewer pub. Just down the A537 towards Macclesfield is the Cock Inn.

Visitor Attractions

LITTLE LEIGH is a small village with the delightful church of St Michael and All Angels COMBERBACH is also on the route and has the interestingly named pubs The Spinner and Bergamot and The Drum and Monkey Marbury Country Park about a mile to the south has toilets, a picnic area and an arboretum and community orchard

THE ANDERTON BOAT LIFT Remarkable feat of Victorian engineering built to get boats up and down the 50feet between the River Weaver and the Trent & Mersey Canal Viewing area, cafe, shop and toilets but also guided trips through the lift and boat trips (charges for these) 🚲 just over a mile

LION SALT WORKS Ollershaw Lane Marston CW9 6ES (01606 41823) 💻 www.lionsaltworkstrust.co.uk Open-pan saltworks open Sunday to Thursday 1.30 - 4.30 Donation suggested for admission 🚲 about 1.5 miles

GREAT BUDWORTH Make sure you've got a camera - extraordinarily pretty village with timber-framed houses, an ancient church and the old and picturesque George and Dragon 🚲 on the route

ARLEY HALL AND GARDENS AND STOCKLEY FARM See day ride

HIGH LEGH is in beautiful countryside and has a garden centre with a coffee shop

ROSTHERNE is a delightful village of estate type buildings and has the deepest mere in Cheshire nearby, home to a huge variety of wild birds and reputedly a mermaid, although to visit the mere you need a permit (English Nature) Good view of it from the churchyard

TATTON PARK Knutsford WA16 6QN (01625 534400) 💻 www.tattonpark.org.uk Main hall, Tudor Old Hall, deer, Stable restaurant and cycle hire (01827 284646 www.cyclelinehire.co.uk) Free entry to the parkland for walkers and cyclists 🚲 The main hall and restaurant is about 1 mile off the route south of Rostherne

KNUTSFORD is only about three miles from the Cycleway at various points and is probably most nicely approached by riding down through Tatton Park It has some highly distinctive architecture giving it an atmosphere all of its own and is the Cranford of Mrs. Gaskell The Knutsford Heritage Centre (01565 650506) is built on the site of a former smithy and is open daily See the penny farthing bicycle collection at the Courtyard Coffee House MOBBERLEY lies between the Cheshire Cycleway and the eastern side of Knutsford

ALDERLEY EDGE Pleasant town with a good range of shops and the neighbouring 600feet sandstone escarpment which has been home to copper mining and stories of wizards and is now a popular National Trust area of woodland walks and fine views across Cheshire For refreshments see The Wizard Tearoom under Food and Drink 🚲 the town is about a mile from the Cycleway, the Edge less

NETHER ALDERLEY MILL Congleton Road Nether Alderley (01625 584412) is a National Trust 15th century mill restored to working order and with an original Victorian waterwheel Flour grinding demonstrations are held regularly See www.nationaltrust.org.uk or phone for opening arrangements Admission charge to non-members 🚲 0.3 miles

HARE HILL at Over Alderley is National Trust parkland with woodland grounds and a walled garden Great displays of rhododendrons and azaleas Open late March to late October - see www.nationaltrust.org.uk or tel (01625 584412) for days and times Admission charge to non-members 🚲 on route

CAPESTHORNE HALL is about two miles west of the Cheshire Cycleway link The magnificent hall and grounds are open two days a week plus bank holidays from April to October inclusive (admission charge) Refreshments available in the Butler's Pantry See www.capesthorne.com or tel (01625 861221) for further details Nearby is the delightful REDESMERE lake, great for birdwatchers and used by fishermen and sailors but also just very pretty HENBURY HALL, adjacent to this section of the Cycleway, is only open for group visits booked in advance

PRESTBURY Nothing remarkable in the way of facilities, although some nice pubs and eating places, but what a pretty village ⛲ on the route

BOLLINGTON Small, quiet place with shops and places to eat On the other side of the town to the Cycleway is the Macclesfield Canal with the magnificent Adelphi and Clarence Mills standing on its banks Clarence Mill contains the Bollington Discovery Centre which tells you all about the history of the town and the canal - open at weekends The White Nancy monument overlooks Bollington from Kerridge Hill and was probably built to commemorate Waterloo 🚰 town centre just off the route

Pennine architecture awaits you at Bollington

Bike Shops

Dave Hinde Cycles 227 Manchester Rd Northwich CW9 7NB 01606 48608 🚲2.5 miles
Bikes 'n' Gear 31 King St Knutsford WA16 6DW 01565 750273 🚲3 miles
Bikes 80 Park Lane Macclesfield SK11 6UA 01625 611375 🚲1.5 to 2 miles depending on route

Tourist Information

Northwich TIC 1 Market Arcade Northwich CW9 5AS 01606 353534
💻 www.valeroyal.gov.uk
Knutsford TIC Council Offices Toft Road Knutsford WA16 6TA 01565 632611
💻 www.macclesfield.gov.uk
Macclesfield TIC Town Hall SK10 1DX 01625 504114 💻As Knutsford

Quiet roads in Tatton Park

3 Bollington - Marton

Route Info

20 miles / 32 km
Off - road 0 miles / 0 km
Height Ascended 506m / 1661ft

A hugely impressive section of towering scenery but with long and serious gradients to match as you climb steeply out of Bollington into the Peak District proper. This area of 'the Peak' is particularly challenging to cyclists as the hills rise and fall like waves, one after another. The rewards are views over some spectacularly shaped hills and Lamaload Reservoir before one of the best views in Cheshire at the ancient cross just south of Macclesfield Forest. Planes at Manchester Airport take off and land below you and the views stretch for miles and miles across the Cheshire Plain.

The long run down through Wildboarclough

A - B

From the Crown in Bollington head up Church St. and pass the church on your L. At the mini-roundabout bear R then immediate R onto Ingersley Rd. This becomes a long hard climb of around 1.5 miles to the B5470 (ignore the L to Pott Shrigley on the way). Jink R then L over the B road and pass the R turn to Common Barn Farm. Bear R at the next two junctions to pass Lamaload Reservoir and climb steeply to the A537.

B - C

Head S/O here and continue to the Stanley Arms pub where you turn R, signed Forest Chapel, Wildboarclough and Wincle. There follows a lovely, long downhill run of around 2.5 miles to Wildboarclough which is over the small bridge on your L, signed for Buxton. The Cheshire Cycleway carries on, on the same road, passing the Crag Inn to take the next R turn by a bungalow. After this turn follow the road for around 1.5 miles to come to a T-junction where you turn R past the Hanging Gate pub. Descend and hairpin L to Higher Sutton and simply continue, ignoring all minor turnings, into Sutton Lane Ends. Turn L and immediate L again by Church House pub, signed Sutton / Lyme Green. At the staggered crossroads head across Hall Lane onto Walker Lane (Lamb Inn on the L).

Crown copyright and/or database right. All rights reserved. Licence number 100040135

DIRECTIONS NOT

R = right

L = left

S/O = straight ov

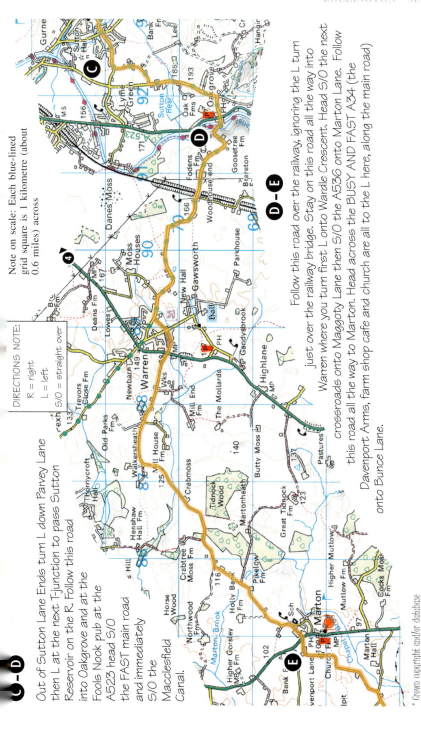

C – D

Out of Sutton Lane Ends turn L down Parvey Lane then L at the next Tjunction to pass Sutton Reservoir on the R. Follow this road into Oakgrove and at the Fools Nook pub at the A523 head S/O the FAST main road and immediately S/O the Macclesfield Canal.

Follow this road over the railway, ignoring the L turn just over the railway bridge. Stay on this road all the way into Warren where you turn first L onto Wardle Crescent. Head S/O the next crossroads onto Maggoty Lane then S/O the A536 onto Marton Lane. Follow this road all the way to Marton. Head across the BUSY AND FAST A34 (the Davenport Arms, farm shop cafe and church are all to the L here, along the main road) onto Bunce Lane.

DIRECTIONS NOTE:
R = right
L = left
S/O = straight over

Note on scale: Each blue-lined grid square is 1 kilometre (about 0.6 miles) across

D – E

* Crown copyright and/or database right. All rights reserved. Licence number 100040155

Hotels and Guesthouses

BOLLINGTON TO MARTON

❶COMMON BARN FARM Bed and Breakfast and Self Catering Cottages Smith Lane Rainow Macclesfield SK10 5XJ (01625 574878) 💻www.cottages-with-a-view.co.uk From £28.00 🛏5d1triple1t all en suite with a disabled room with en suite wet room   Stars and diamonds rating and listed with Tourist Information Centre   🍴 tearoom available for light snacks and lunches 🍴 ⛳ ▫ 🚲 ✗ Pressure hose for bike washing 🚌 possible if fairly local   Set on a working hill sheep farm Self catering in 4 star cottages also available   🚶half a mile

❷ THE ROSE AND CROWN INN Allgreave Wildboarclough SK11 0BJ (01260 227232) 💻www.theroseandcrown.net   £27.50   🛏2d1t all en suite   ♦♦♦ 🍴 restaurant open every lunchtime and evening 🍴 from £3.50 ⛳ 🚲   Open all year 🚶0.8 miles

❸ THE RYLES ARMS Hollin Lane Higher Sutton Macclesfield SK11 0NN (01260 252244)   💻info@rylesarms.com   From £30.00   🛏1f3d1t   ♦♦♦♦ Tourist Information Centre listed   🍴full menu available for lunch and dinner   🍴2 hours notice ⛳drying room ▫laundry room ✗ 🚲   Open 365 days a year   🚶1.5 miles

❹ PREMIER TRAVEL INN Congleton Road Gawsworth SK11 7XD (0870 9906412)   💻www.premiertravelinn.com   Room only £46.95 - £48.95 🍴 Breakfast from £5.25 (Millers pub & restaurant next door)   🚶1.5 miles

The quiet but steep roads above Bollington near Nab End

The ancient cross south of Macclesfield Forest gives superb views over the Cheshire Plain

Hostels and Campsites

BOLLINGTON TO MARTON

① COMMON BARN FARM Smith Lane Rainow Macclesfield SK10 5XJ (01625 574878) ⌨www.cottages-with-a-view.co.uk Λ ⛺Half a mile

② TORGATE FARM Macclesfield Forest SK11 0AR (01260 252392) Λ £2.00 per person per night (£5.00 pppn caravans) Flush toilet Cold water Open all year ⛺0.5 miles

③ BERRY BANK FARM Wildboarclough SK11 0BG (01260 227280) Λ Toilets Open most of the year The Crag Inn and the Rose and Crown pubs nearby do food ⛺ about 1 mile

④ UNDERBANK CAMPING BARN Blaze Farm Wildboarclough Macclesfield SK11 0BL (01260 227229 or 227266) ⌨www.yha.org.uk Accommodates up to ten Breakfast available There is a cafe and ice cream parlour nearby on the farm Λtent camping also available and a self-catering holiday cottage 🍽 with notice 🚲 ⛺ 1.2 miles

⑤ THE ROSE AND CROWN INN Allgreave Wildboarclough SK11 0BJ (01260 227232) ⌨www.theroseandcrown.net Λ Toilet facilities Open all year ⛺ 0.8 miles

⑥YHA GRADBACH Gradbach Mill Gradbach Quarnford SK17 0SU (0870 7705834) www.yha.org.uk 🏳 🚲 ⛺3.2 miles

⑦ JARMAN FARM Jarman Road Sutton SK11 0HJ (01260 252501) Λ Toilets and showers Camping and Caravanning Club site Primarily for caravans so tent pitches subject to availability Open summer only ⛺Near route

41

Gawsworth Hall

Food and Drink Suggestions

Note: The listings below are not comprehensive.
See red symbols on maps for the location of even more cafes (🍽) and pubs (P)

COMMON BARN FARM Smith Lane Rainow Macclesfield SK10 5XJ (01625 574878)
🖳www.cottages-with-a-view.co.uk   Tearoom open 10.00 - 5.00 daily all year round except
Mondays and Christmas Day and New Year's Day   Light snacks and lunches   🚲Half a mile

On the route are the STANLEY ARMS at Bottom-of-the-Oven and the CRAG INN &
BROOKSIDE CAFE at Wildboarclough

BLAZE FARM ICE CREAM PARLOUR AND CAFE Wildboarclough Nr. Macclesfield (01260
227229 or 227266) 🖳www.blazefarm.com   Range of snacks, drinks and ice creams
🚲1.2 miles

THE ROSE AND CROWN INN Allgreave Wildboarclough SK11 0BJ (01260 227232)
🖳www.theroseandcrown.net   Bar snacks to full meals including specials and vegetarian
Open every lunchtime and evening   🚲0.6 miles

THE RYLES ARMS Hollin Lane Higher Sutton SK11 0NN (01260 252244)
🖳info@rylesarms.com Open 12.00 noon to 11.00pm Range of dishes starting from £3.95
🚲   🚲1.5 miles

THE DAVENPORT ARMS Manchester Road (A34) Marton SK11 9HF   (01260 224269)
🖳sara@thedavenportarms.co.uk   Snacks, full meals and a la carte available 12.00 - 2.30
and 6.00 - 9.00 daily except Mondays   🚲   🚲almost on route

THE BLACK SWAN Trap Street Lower Withington SK11 9EQ (01477 571602) Traditional
meals, sandwiches and a la carte £5.00 - £10.00 for full meal and drink   Food 12.00 - 2.00
and 6.00 - 9.30 🚲1.4 miles

Visitor Attractions

MACCLESFIELD is a very pleasant town, ringed by the Cheshire Cycleway and the centre is only a couple of miles or so from the route to the north or the south It has decent shops and eating places and three of the four museums show the town's involvement in the silk industry - see www.macclesfield .silk.museum for opening times, admission prices and further information The West Park Museum (non-silk) is in the same park as what is reportedly England's largest crown bowling green Interesting walks alongside the Macclesfield Canal which runs close to the town

MACCLESFIELD FOREST Large area of forest, reservoirs and moorland with waymarked walks and mountain bike routes Visitor information and toilets at the Trentabank Reservoir car park   Mountain bike map for Macclesfield Forest and Wildboarclough available from Finders UK Ltd Ruskin Chambers Drury Lane Knutsford WA16 6HA (Tel 01565 750049) edge of forest almost up to route, Trentabank about 1.5 miles

WILDBOARCLOUGH has no real centre but has a magnificent private house which used to be part of a mill and was then used as a post office, the largest sub post office in the country apparently. Nearby is the church and on the bridge a plaque commemorates a bad flood in 1989   Also not far away is the 506 metre Shutlingslowe from which there are excellent views

TEGG'S NOSE COUNTRY PARK Buxton Old Road Macclesfield SK11 0DG Country park with picnic area and toilets It's also the start of Regional Route 71 (see pages 158-159) one and a half miles

SUTTON LANE ENDS has pubs serving food and restaurants including The Ryles Arms (see under Food and Drink) The Macclesfield Canal passes the village about a kilometre from the route   Further on the canal is crossed by the route at OAKGROVE where there is the Fool's Nook Inn

GAWSWORTH HALL Church Lane Gawsworth SK11 9RN (01260 223456) www.gawsworthhall.com   Half timbered late fifteenth century manor house. Fully furnished and lived in by the family Open April to September (telephone for opening days and times) Closed end September to Easter   Cafe   Open Air Theatre Festival end June to mid-August Craft Fairs Spring and August Bank Holidays   Classic Car Show first May Bank Holiday Monday   0.25 miles

JODRELL BANK VISITOR CENTRE Macclesfield SK11 9DL (01477 571339) www.manchester.ac.uk/jodrellbank/viscen   Home of the Lovell Radio Telescope   Take a journey to Mars or tour the solar system in the 3D theatre   Explore the seasons in the 35 acre arboretum with national collections of Malus and Sorbus   Picnic areas   Shop   Cafe Open all year - mid March to last Sunday in October is 10.30 - 5.30 daily and November to mid March is Tuesday to Friday 10.30 - 3.00 and Saturday and Sunday 11.00 - 4.00 Both hot and cold food and drinks are available in the cafe   Cycle racks close to the visitor centre   4 miles

MARTON is a small village but it does have the Davenport Arms (see Food and Drink for details) and a farm shop and cafe just south on the A34 The small black and white church here is quaint and worth a look

View from the route east of Bollington

Bike Shops

Bikes 80 Park Lane Macclesfield SK11 6UA 01625 611375 🚲1.5 to 2 miles depending on route

Tourist Information

Macclesfield TIC Town Hall SK10 1DX 01625 504114 💻www.macclesfield.gov.uk

Many villages in Cheshire have unique signs reflecting their character and history

4 Marton - Malpas

Route Info

43 miles / 69 km
Off - road 1.3 miles / 2km
Height Ascended 569m / 1866ft

After crossing the meandering River Dane you skirt Congleton before coming to a series of beautiful villages including Barthomley, Weston and Wybunbury. Beautiful Audlem is Cheshire's most southerly town and a visit to the canal wharf, with its locks and cheery pubs is a must. More idyllic villages and another canal crossing await as you pass through Aston, Wrenbury and Marbury. The hilltop town of Malpas with its many shops and collection of characterful buildings is a fine finish to this section and worth taking time to explore.

Near Newsbank

45

A - B

Heading away from Marton on Bunce Lane turn R at the next T-junction. Bear L at the next junction and follow Mill Lane. At the T-junction in Newsbank turn R, signed Somerford, Swettenham & Lower Withington (L is NCN route 55 to Hulme Walfield and Congleton). Take the next L onto Hallgreen Lane, signed Somerford & Swettenham. Pass Swettenham Rd and cross the River Dane to split onto Black Firs Lane. At the A54 turn L then immediate R, signed Newcastle A34 & Nantwich A534, onto Box Lane. Cross S/O the A534 onto Padgbury Lane. At the A34 turn R WITH CARE (Astbury Mere is S/O here). The A34 takes you past the lovely village of Astbury on the L; definitely worth a look.

B - C

Take the next R, signed Brownlow & Smallwood, onto Childs Lane. Follow this road for about 2.7 miles, past the Bluebell Inn and through Smallwood. S/O the A50, signed Betchton & Hassall Green.

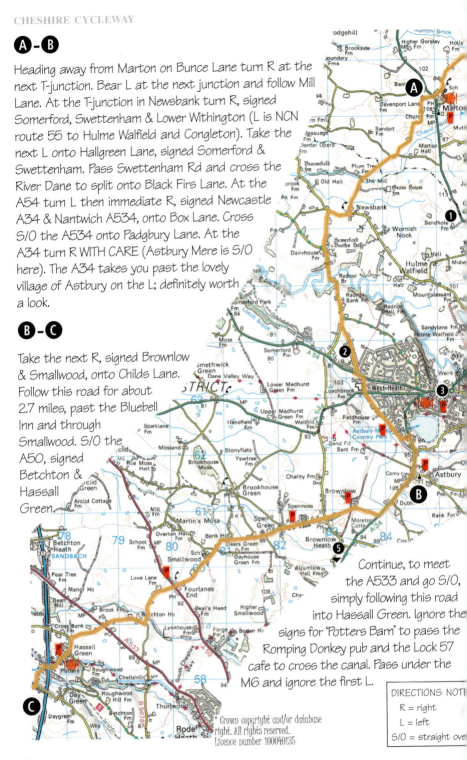

Continue, to meet the A533 and go S/O, simply following this road into Hassall Green. Ignore the signs for 'Potters Barn' to pass the Romping Donkey pub and the Lock 57 cafe to cross the canal. Pass under the M6 and ignore the first L.

DIRECTIONS NOTE
R = right
L = left
S/O = straight ove

Crown copyright and/or database right. All rights reserved. Licence number 100040135

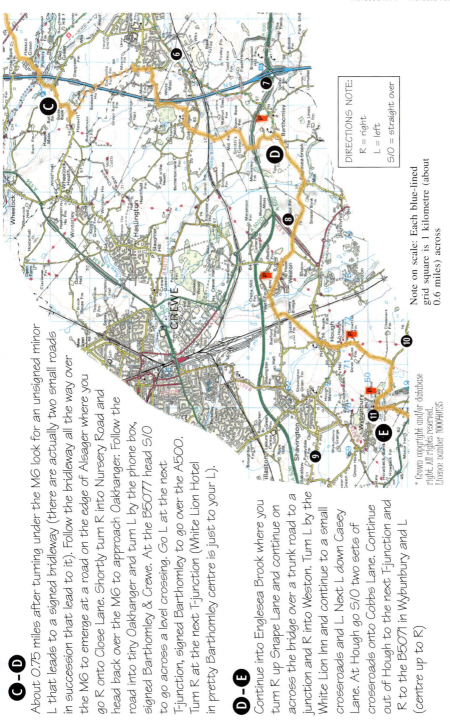

DIRECTIONS NOTE:
R = right
L = left
S/O = straight over

Note on scale: Each blue-lined grid square is 1 kilometre (about 0.6 miles) across

* Crown copyright and/or database right. All rights reserved.
Licence number 100040735

C – D

About 0.75 miles after turning under the M6 look for an unsigned minor L that leads to a signed bridleway (there are actually two small roads in succession that lead to it). Follow the bridleway all the way over the M6 to emerge at a road on the edge of Alsager where you go R onto Close Lane. Shortly turn R into Nursery Road and head back over the M6 to approach Oakhanger. Follow the road into tiny Oakhanger and turn L by the phone box, signed Barthomley & Crewe. At the B5077 head S/O to go across a level crossing. Go L at the next T-junction, signed Barthomley to go over the A500. Turn R at the next T-junction (White Lion Hotel in pretty Barthomley centre is just to your L).

D – E

Continue into Englesea Brook where you turn R up Snape Lane and continue on across the bridge over a trunk road to a junction and R into Weston. Turn L by the White Lion Inn and continue to a small crossroads and L. Next L down Casey Lane. At Hough go S/O two sets of crossroads onto Cobbs Lane. Continue out of Hough to the next T-junction and R to the B5071 in Wybunbury and L (centre up to R)

47

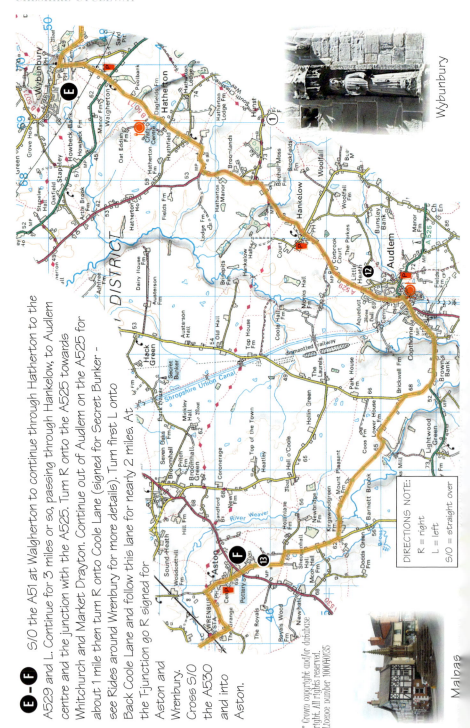

Wybunbury

Malpas

E - F S/O the A51 at Walgherton to continue through Hatherton to the A529 and L. Continue for 3 miles or so, passing through Hankelow, to Audlem centre and the junction with the A525. Turn R onto the A525 towards Whitchurch and Market Drayton. Continue out of Audlem on the A525 for about 1 mile then turn R onto Coole Lane (signed for Secret Bunker – see Rides around Wrenbury for more details). Turn first L onto Back Coole Lane and follow this lane for nearly 2 miles. At the T-junction go R signed for Aston and Wrenbury. Cross S/O the A530 and into Aston.

DIRECTIONS NOTE:
R = right
L = left
S/O = straight over

* Crown copyright and/or database right. All rights reserved.
Licence number 100040035

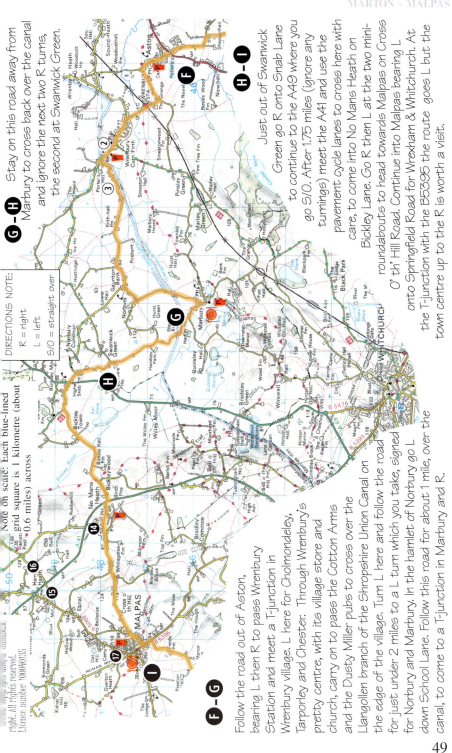

right. All rights reserved.
Licence number 100040135

Note on scale: Each blue-lined grid square is 1 kilometre (about 0.6 miles) across

DIRECTIONS NOTE:
R = right
L = left
S/O = straight over

G – H Stay on this road away from Marbury to cross back over the canal and ignore the next two R turns, the second at Swanwick Green.

H – I Just out of Swanwick Green go R onto Snab Lane to continue to the A49 where you go S/O. After 1.75 miles (ignore any turnings) meet the A41 and use the pavement cycle lanes to cross here with care, to come into No Mans Heath on Bickley Lane. Go R then L at the two mini-roundabouts to head towards Malpas on Cross O' th' Hill Road. Continue into Malpas bearing L onto Springfield Road for Wrexham & Whitchurch. At the T-junction with the B5395 the route goes L but the town centre up to the R is worth a visit.

F – G Follow the road out of Aston, bearing L then R to pass Wrenbury Station and meet a T-junction in Wrenbury village. L here for Cholmondeley, Tarporley and Chester: Through Wrenbury's pretty centre, with its village store and church, carry on to pass the Cotton Arms and the Dusty Miller pubs to cross over the Llangollen branch of the Shropshire Union Canal on the edge of the village. Turn L here and follow the road for just under 2 miles to a L turn which you take, signed for Norbury and Marbury. In the hamlet of Norbury go L down School Lane. Follow this road for about 1 mile, over the canal, to come to a T-junction in Marbury and R.

49

Hotels and Guesthouses

MARTON TO MALPAS

❶ SANDHOLE FARM A34 Manchester Road Hulme Walfield Congleton CW12 2JH (01260 224419) www.sandholefarm.co.uk £31.00 5d1s3f6t ♦♦♦♦ Tourist Information Centre listed Flask filling tumble dryer, radiators Open all year including Christmas (D.I.Y. breakfasts at Christmas) 1.3 miles

❷ COPPICE EDGE Bed & Breakfast Blackfirs Lane Somerford CW12 4QQ (01260 270605) www.coppice-edge.co.uk £25.00 1d/tr en suite 1s1dwith private facilities ♦♦♦♦ Tourist Information Centre listed drying room Bike washing facilities possible Open all year on the route

❸ THE LAMB INN 3 Blake Street Congleton CW12 4DS (01260 272731) www.lambinn.org.uk £20.00 standard £22.00 en suite 1s 3d/t en suite 2f en suite close to town centre restaurants and public houses Flask and bottle filling available at no charge all rooms have radiators Hose for bike washing Open all year adjacent to A34, 1 mile to cycleway

❹ THE LION AND SWAN Swan Bank Congleton CW12 1AH (01260 273115) www.lionandswan.co.uk From £30.00 22 rooms - standard, executive, family ★★★ Tourist Information Centre listed lunch and evening meal available in restaurant 1.5 miles, near town centre

❺ CUTTLEFORD FARM Astbury Congleton CW12 4SD (01260 272499) £24.00 - £30.00 1d1t 1en suite Open all year 1.2 miles

❻ HOLLY TREES HOTEL Crewe Road Alsager ST7 2JL (01270 876847) www.hollytreeshotel.co.uk £27.50 6d2s1t1f ♦♦♦♦ Tourist Information Centre listed evening meals available £5.95 tumble dryer £5.00 a load Open all year round - 365 days including Christmas and New Year 0.7 miles

❼ TRAVELODGE Junction 16 M6/A500 Alsager Road Barthomley CW2 5PT (0870 1911571) www.travelodge.co.uk Little Chef & Burger King nearby 1.25 miles

❽ SNAPE FARM Snape Lane Weston CW2 5NB (01270 820208) jean@snapefarm.fsnet.co.uk on the route

❾ OAKLAND HOUSE 252 Newcastle Road Blakelow Nantwich CW5 7ET (01270 567134) enquiries@oaklandhouse.co.uk £27.00 5d3t1f1s ♦♦♦♦♦ Tourist Information Centre listed £5.00 use of washer and dryer Fridge available to store fresh food and cold drinks Open all year 2 miles

❿ LEA FARM Wrinehill Road Wybunbury CW5 7NS (01270 841429) www.smoothhound.co.uk/hotels/leafarm £23.00 - £26.00 1f1t1d1s ♦♦♦ Tourist Information Centre listed salad meals available 12 hours notice drying facilities, also central heating in cold weather by arrangement Power washing for bikes Open all year 0.5 miles

⓫ THE SWAN INN 2 Main Road Wybunbury CW5 5RP (01270 841280) £32.50 2f2d2t All rooms are en suite with television AA rated and Tourist Information Centre listed lunch and evening meals available - see food and drink entry for details when possible tumble dryer and radiators Hose available for bike washing Open all year on the cycleway

⑫ BERRY COTTAGE Ivy House Monks Lane Audlem CW3 0HP   (01270 811573) ⌨hardwork@tesco.net   Self catering cottage   £25.00 per person per night   🛏1d1s ★★★★   Tourist Information Centre listed   🍽 light breakfast provided   👕 tumble dryer ▫ washer   🚲 Hose available for washing bikes   Open all year including Christmas etc. 🚶half a mile

⑬ BRIAR COTTAGE Sheppenhall Lane Aston CW5 8DE (01270 781288) ⌨www.briarcottageaston.com   £27.50 - £30.00   🛏2d1s all en suite   Tourist Information Centre listed   👕drying room   🚲   🚌   Open all year   🚶on the cycleway

⑭ MILLMOOR FARM HOLIDAYS Millmoor Farm No Man's Heath Malpas SY14 8DY (01948 820304) ⌨www.millmoorfarm.co.uk   £20.00 - £25.00   🛏1four poster family en suite 1d en suite 1tprivate bathroom   ♦♦♦♦   Tourist Information Centre listed   🍽 two course evening meal £10.00   🍽 £3.50 one day notice   👕radiators all year Tumble dryer also   ▫washing machine   🚌 sometimes available   🚲   hose available for bike washing   Open all year including Christmas and New Year   Four star self catering cottage to sleep four also avail- able   Coarse fishing available   Good pub meals within walking distance (one mile) 🚶0.5 miles

⑮ HAMILTON HOUSE BED & BREAKFAST Station Road Hampton Heath Malpas SY14 8JF (01948 820421) ⌨hamiltonhouse5@hotmail.com   En suite room high season £25.50, low season £24.00Room with bathroom £24.00 high season, £22.50 low season   🛏1t 1d en suite 1t 1s with bathroom   ♦♦♦   Tourist Information Centre listed   🍽 pub within walking distance but can offer lift to Wheatsheaf in No Mans Heath   🍽   👕 around range in kitchen or log burner   ▫   🚲   🔧   Hosepipe for bike washing   🚌   🚶1.5 miles

⑯ HAMPTON HOUSE FARM Stevensons Lane Hampton Malpas SY14 8JS (01948 820588) ⌨www.hamptonhousefarm.co.uk   £25.00   ♦♦♦♦   Tourist Information Centre listed 🍽 24 hours notice £3.50   👕clothes airer in front of boiler   🚲   🔧   Pressure washer for washing bikes Open all year   🚶1.7 miles

⑰ WESTLEIGH 163 High Street Malpas SY14 8PR (01948 860124 / 07773 438053) ⌨ctroika@aol.com   £38.00-40.00 high season   Tourist Information Centre listed   🍽   👕   ▫ 🚲   Closed Christmas only   🚶0.25 miles

View from the Cheshire Cycleway approaching Wybunbury

Hostels and Campsites

MARTON TO MALPAS

① FOXES BANK FARM Hunsterson CW5 7PN (01270 520224)   ▲   Toilets and a shower Open all year   🚶0.6 miles

② COTTON ARMS Cholmondeley Road Wrenbury CW5 8HG (01270 780377) ⌨www.caravancampingsites.co.uk/cheshire/cottonarms.htm   ▲ £8.00 a pitch   Toilets and showers   Pub has restaurant and does take-away food   Food shop nearby   🚲   Open all year 🚶on the route

③ 1, BELMONT VILLA Frith Lane Wrenbury CW5 8HQ (01270 780366)   ▲ Certificated Location for touring caravans which takes tents also No facilities Open most of the year   🚶on the route

Food and Drink Suggestions

Note: The listings below are not comprehensive.
See red symbols on maps for the location of even more cafes (🍽) and pubs (🍺)

THE LION AND SWAN Swan Bank Congleton CW12 1AH (01260 273115)
🖥 www.lionandswan.co.uk   Bar snacks, table d'hote and a la carte Sandwiches etc. £3.95
Three course table d'hote £10.95   Breakfast 7.00 - 9.00 (10.00 weekends) Lunch 12.00 -
2.30 Dinner 5.30 - 9.00 Bar open all day   🚲   🚶1.5 miles, near Congleton town
centre

THE BULLS HEAD Newcastle Road Smallwood near Sandbach CW11 2TY (01477
500247) 🖥 www.thebullsheadatsmallwood.co.uk   Range of food is traditional English,
homemade and classical Full range of bar snacks at all times Price range for full meal and
drink is over £10.00   Open all day 12.00 - 11.00 (10.30 Sunday) with food being served
12.00 - 9.30   Posts and benches to secure bikes to   🚶0.4 miles

THE NEW INN Newcastle Road Betchton Sandbach CW11 2TG (01477 500237)
🖥 markatthenewinn@aol.com   Traditional English fayre Also meals from around the world
Full lunchtime menu 12.00 - 2.30, full evening menu 5.30 - 9.30 Price range for full meal
and drink £5.00 - £10.00 🚲   Friendly atmosphere Everybody welcome 🚶on the route

THE ROMPING DONKEY Hassall Road Hassall Green CW11 4YA (01270 765202) Carvery
plus full a la carte vegetarian and snacks Range of prices   Meals served all day from
10.30am to 9.00pm Lots of outside seating available   🚲   🚶on the route

LOCK 57 THE CANAL CENTRE Hassall Green Sandbach CW11 4YB (01270 762266)
Breakfasts, snacks, sandwiches, lunches, Sunday lunches, afternoon tea and evening meals
(a la carte evening menu)   (all traditional English)   Open 9.30 - 4.00 and 6.30 - 11.00
seven days a week Range of prices   Post Office and general store (open 7 days a week) in
the same complex   🚲   🚶on the route

THE RED LION 5 Main Road Road Wybunbury CW5 7NA (01270 842391) Traditional light
snacks Open Monday to Friday 4.00 - 11.00 Saturday/Sunday and Bank Holidays 12.00 -
11.00 Beer garden in suntrap Cask real ales Large screen live sports   🚶On the route

THE SWAN INN 2 Main Road Wybunbury CW5 5RP (01270 841280) Snacks and full meals
Monday 6.30 - 9.30, Tuesday to Saturday 12.00 - 2.00 and 6.30 - 9.30, Sunday and Bank
Holiday Mondays 12.00 - 8.00   Price range for full meal and drink £5.00 - £10.00   🚲
Award winning pub, in the Good Beer guide, CAMRA pub of the year winner   🚶On the
route

BOARS HEAD London Road Walgherton Food all day, every day. 🚶On the route

DAGFIELDS Walgherton - see under visitor attractions

WHITE LION INN Audlem Road Hankelow 🚶On the route

BEAMANS AND THE OLD PRIESTHOUSE COFFEE SHOP 2 Stafford Street Audlem CW3
0AA (01270 811749)   Open 10.00 - 5.00 for full meals English snacks and vegetarian Price
range for full meal and drink £5.00 - £10.00 Cycle rack over the road by the church No
smoking 🚶near the route

THE DUSTY MILLER Wrenbury Nantwich CW5 8HG (01270 780537)   Full meals cooked to
order, many local ingredients, also light bites menu, large selection of British cheeses
Lunch served 12.00 - 2.00, dinner 6.30 - 9.00   Great place to stop, right on the Shropshire
Union Llangollen Canal next to unusual liftbridge River Weaver also passes under canal in
the beer garden   Plenty of things to lock bikes to in the area close to the door
🚶passes the door

There's no better place on a summer's day than The Shroppie Fly at Audlem

CHOLMONDELEY CASTLE FARM SHOP   Castle Farm Complex   Cholmondeley   Malpas   SY14 8AQ   (01829 720201)   Hot and cold snacks and sandwiches on sale Monday to Friday   Cold snacks and sandwiches on sale during weekend opening hours   Cold drinks   All reasonably priced   Open Monday - Friday 8.00 - 6.00 Saturday 8.00 - 12.30 and Sunday 9.00 - 6.00 in summer and 9.00 - 4.00 October - pre-Easter   Picnic bench   🚶1.6 miles

CREATION STATION   The Former Fire Station   High Street   Malpas   SY14 8NR   (01948 860989)   Sandwiches, toasties, light snacks, beans on toast etc, flapjacks and muffins   Freshly ground coffee and other drinks   Meal and drink for under £5.00   See Attractions for opening hours   🚶near the route

Visitor Attractions

CONGLETON is only about a mile from the Cycleway   A signed, mainly on-road route, Regional Route 73 goes in to the town from the Cycleway through West Heath Plenty of shops and places to stay, eat, drink or be entertained Covered market open Tuesdays and Saturdays The bear on the town crest is said to derive from bear-baiting days when the town bear died and money set aside for a new town bible was used to buy a new bear

ASTBURY MERE COUNTRY PARK Sandy Lane Congleton CW12 4FR   (01260 297237) ⌨astbury@cheshire.gov.uk   Ten hectares of open space with panoramic views over Astbury Mere and the surrounding countryside Visitor centre Toilets   Cycle rack Outdoor seating Easy access trail and orienteering course   Open 24hours / 7 days a week all year Visitor centre 9.00 - 5.00 daily   🚲0.5 miles

THE NATIONAL TRUST LITTLE MORETON HALL Congleton CW12 4SD (01260 272018) ⌨www.nationaltrust.org.uk   Little Moreton Hall is Britain's most famous and arguably finest timber-framed manor house The drunkenly reeling south front, topped by a spectacular long gallery, opens onto a cobbled courtyard and the main body of the hall Magnificent wall paintings and a notable knot garden are of special interest   Phone or see website for opening days and times Shop Restaurant   Admission free to National Trust members Non-members £5.25 adults, £2.80 children, £12.50 family (during Yuletide children free and adults £2.00) Dedicated area of car park for cycles   🚲1.25 miles

SANDBACH can be reached easily from the trail along a traffic-free section of NCN5 from Hassall Green and then by road into the town where there is a cycle lane running through the town centre Worth a visit not least for the dramatic Anglo-Saxon stone crosses in Market Place There are several hotels in Sandbach, main bank branches and plenty of shops (including a market hall) and places to eat and drink. Information centre in the library. 🚲about 2 miles

The route crosses the Trent & Mersey canal at HASSALL GREEN, a pretty spot with the Romping Donkey and Lock 57 (see Food and Drink for details), a shop and post office and the Potter's Barn pottery

ALSAGER can be reached on NCN 5 from Hassall Green or on the traffic-free Salt Line from just south of Hassall Green and then on-road into the town centre

BARTHOMLEY is a lovely-looking village with black and white timbered buildings and the White Lion pub

ENGLESEA BROOK CHAPEL AND MUSEUM Englesea Brook Lane Englesea Brook CW2 5QW (01270 820836) Early 19th century "Ranter" chapel giving a taste of working class religion Museum shop Video presentations, magic lantern show, children's costumes/dressing up/games and refreshments School visits, local history, the Victorians, working class Sunday school experience Open Thursday, Friday, Saturday and Bank Holiday Monday 10.30 - 5.15 and Sunday 1.30 - 5.15 April to November inclusive and every day except non-Bank Holiday Mondays during August No cafe but do supply tea, coffee, soft drinks and biscuits Admission free Bikes can be padlocked to chapel railings 🚲adjacent to route

Like Barthomley, WESTON has a White Lion, and then for variety, HOUGH has a White Hart

WYBUNBURY has the Red Lion and the Swan (see other sections for details) and is a delightful village with its church tower something of a landmark - the rest of the church had to be demolished

DAGFIELDS CRAFT AND ANTIQUE CENTRE Walgherton ⌨www.dagfields.co.uk (01270 841336) Open daily Tearooms and cafe as well as antiques and crafts 🚲on the route

AUDLEM   A fine country town with bags of charm due to its splendid central church, wide range of local shops (its a good place to stock up on food, grab a coffee or even a bag of chips) and a great stretch of canal alongside which lie two lovely pubs. One, The Shroppie Fly, is named after the old fly-boats, fast horse-drawn water buses that once plyed their trade along the Shropshire Union Canal.

HACK GREEN NUCLEAR BUNKER off French Lane Hack Green Nantwich CW5 8AQ (01270 629219)   www.hackgreen.co.uk   Underground bunker, declassified in 1993, which would have been the centre of regional government in the event of nuclear war Open daily late March to end of October and weekends and half terms otherwise, although closed during December   Cafe   Now well signposted Admission charge   about 2 miles

WRENBURY, set around the village green, has a village store and post office, a brewery and various other services including some fine canal-side pubs (see Food and Drink for the Dusty Miller) The railway station is on the line between Crewe and Nantwich one way and Whitchurch, Prees, Wem, Yorton and Shrewsbury the other

CHOLMONDELEY CASTLE GARDENS Malpas SY14 8AH (01829 720383)   Extensive parkland and variety of gardens   Open April - end September Wednesday, Thursday, Sunday and bank holidays Admission charge   a good 2 miles

NO MANS HEATH, just before Malpas, has a sculpture commemmorating the travels of a seventeenth century lady, Celia Fiennes, although she probably didn't get as far as her modern day relative Sir Ranulph   More of a small town than a village, MALPAS is an excellent place to break with plenty of shops, places to eat and accommodation

CREATION STATION The Former Fire Station High Street Malpas SY14 8NR   (01948 860989) Pottery painting and coffee shop Open 10.00 - 4.30 Monday, Tuesday, Friday and Saturday and 11.00 - 4.30 Sunday Open all year with extra hours during school holidays   near the route

Audlem centre

Many Cheshire villages are packed with colour - as at Wrenbury stores and post office

Bike Shops - Marton to Malpas

Cycle Centre 36-40 West Road Congleton CW12 ES 01260 297837 about one mile

Deans Toys & Cycles 30 Lawton Street Congleton CW12 1RT 01260 273277
 1.75 miles

Tourist Information

Congleton TIC Town Hall High Street Congleton CW12 1BN (01260 271095)
www.congletonarea.com www.visitchester.com

Nantwich TIC Church House Church Walk Nantwich CW5 5RG (01270 610983)
www.crewe-nantwich.gov.uk www.visitchester.com

5 Malpas - Chester

Route Info

33 miles / 53 km
Off - road   2.5 miles / 4 km
Height Ascended   402m / 1318ft

As you pass along very quiet lanes through sleepy Threapwood and Shocklach there is little hint of the dramatic scenery ahead of you in the form of the Peckforton Hills, with their steep sandstone sides cloaked in woods and topped by castles and an ancient Iron Age fort site. Add to this the truly memorable views back to Beeston Castle from Wharton's Lock and an easy-going towpath approach on good quality path into the historic heart of Chester and you have one of the most impressive and varied sections of the Cheshire Cycleway.

ROUTE NOTES Much of this section overlaps or runs near National Cycle Network route 45. Note that this is not the Cheshire Cycleway - the CCW continues to be signed as route 70 and/or the Cheshire Cycleway.

Old and new signs along the route

A – B

Heading south on the B5395 out of Malpas take the R turn on the edge of the town which you follow all the way, through Oldcastle Heath, to Threapwood, some 3.5 miles later. At the first T-junction go R onto Chapel Lane. Shortly meet the T-junction with the B5069 and go L signed Worthenbury (village stores just to the R at this T-junction). Take the first R turn, signed Shocklach and Farndon. Briefly the road passes into Wales on this section (note signs for Wrexham) before coming into the village of Shocklach. Turn R here by the village pub and follow this road out of Shocklach for just over 2 miles, passing through Horton Green, to come to Tilston. Pass St. Mary's Church and the shop/post office and go L by the Carden Arms pub.

B – C

In just over a mile pass Stretton Hall and other fine dwellings. Take the next R here, signed for Stretton Water Mill and Carden. The road runs past a golf course to lovely Stretton Water Mill. Go R by a grand stone entrance lodge, signed for Tilston. L and L again here, signed Duckington and Bickerton.

Cross S/O the BUSY AND FAST A41, signed Duckington and Bickerton. Go R at the T-junction in Duckington and S/O at the crossroads (signed Bickerton). Follow this undulating road through Bickerton and emerge from Goldford Lane by the church on your R and the war memorial on your L. Go L onto Long Lane, signed Broxton. S/O the A534 and follow to a T-junction, going R to climb to Harthill. Next R takes you into Burwardsley. Continue straight on in Burwardsley, passing stores cum post office.

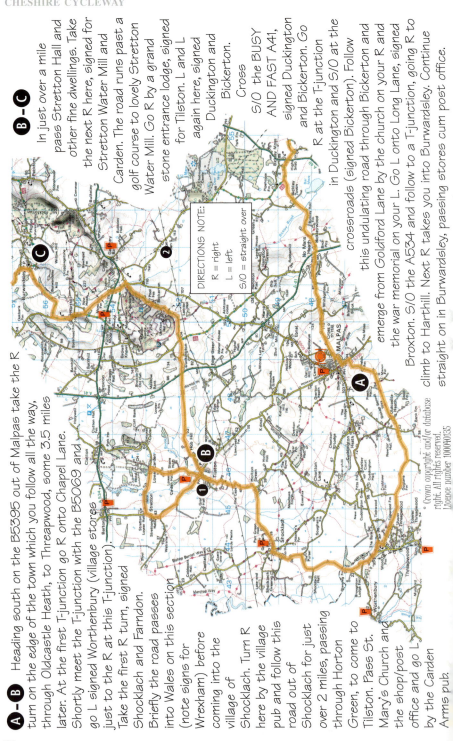

DIRECTIONS NOTE:

R = right
L = left
S/O = straight over

© Crown copyright and/or database right. All rights reserved. Licence number 100040155

DIRECTIONS NOTE:
R = right
L = left
S/O = straight over

D – E

At the next T-junction go R signed for Hargrave, Waverton and Chester. Bear L after Higher Huxley Hall and in about a mile jink over the canal. Stay on this road all the way into Waverton, and past the village hall and school turn R at the junction. Over the canal turn L for Christleton. (Alternatively pick up the canal towpath in Waverton - see overleaf).

Note on scale: Each blue-lined grid square is 1 kilometre (about 0.6 miles) across

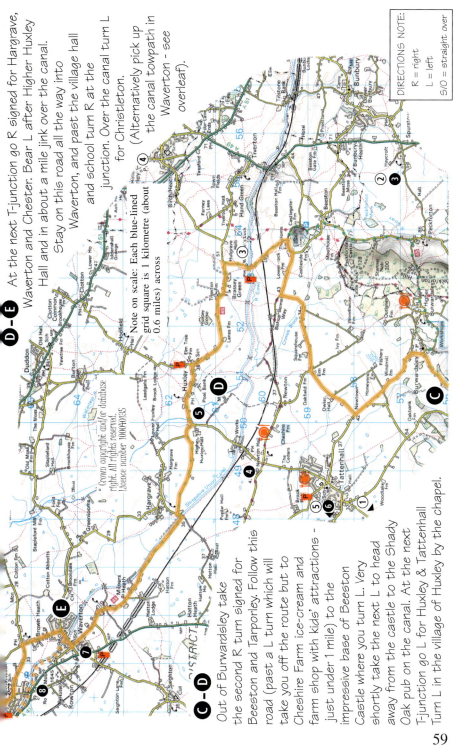

© Crown copyright and/or database right. All rights reserved. Licence number 100040035

C – D

Out of Burwardsley take the second R turn signed for Beeston and Tarporley. Follow this road (past a L turn which will take you off the route but to Cheshire Farm ice-cream and farm shop with kids' attractions - just under 1 mile) to the impressive base of Beeston Castle where you turn L. Very shortly take the next L to head away from the castle to the Shady Oak pub on the canal. At the next T-junction go L for Huxley & Tattenhall. Turn L in the village of Huxley by the chapel.

The Cheshire Cycleway approaching Beeston Castle

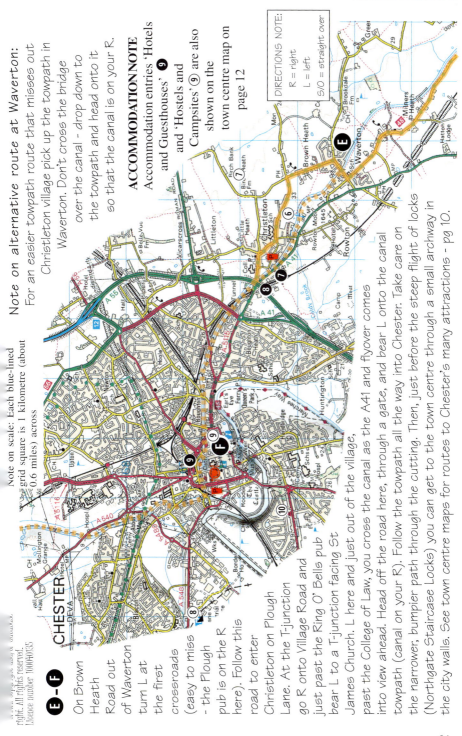

right. All rights reserved.
Licence number 100040035

Note on scale: Each blue-lined grid square is 1 kilometre (about 0.6 miles) across

Note on alternative route at Waverton:

For an easier towpath route that misses out Christleton village pick up the towpath in Waverton. Don't cross the bridge over the canal - drop down to the towpath and head onto it so that the canal is on your R.

ACCOMMODATION NOTE

Accommodation entries 'Hotels and Guesthouses' ❾ and 'Hostels and Campsites' ❾ are also shown on the town centre map on page 12

DIRECTIONS NOTE:
R = right
L = left
S/O = straight over

E - F

On Brown Heath Road out of Waverton turn L at the first crossroads (easy to miss - the Plough pub is on the R here). Follow this road to enter Christleton on Plough Lane. At the T junction go R onto Village Road and just past the Ring O' Bells pub bear L to a T junction facing St James Church. L here and just out of the village, past the College of Law, you cross the canal as the A41 and flyover comes into view ahead. Head off the road here, through a gate, and bear L onto the canal towpath (canal on your R). Follow the towpath all the way into Chester. Take care on the narrower, bumpier path through the cutting. Then, just before the steep flight of locks (Northgate Staircase Locks) you can get to the town centre through a small archway in the city walls. See town centre maps for routes to Chester's many attractions - pg 10.

Hotels and Guesthouses

MALPAS TO CHESTER

❶ TILSTON LODGE   Tilston SY14 7DR   (01829 250223)   £35.00 - £39.00 🛏1t2d (four posters) and one room has extra bed   ♦♦♦♦♦   Tourist Information Centre listed 🍴nominal charge   ⬜   🚲   Launderette in Malpas (3 miles)   Open all year 🚶approx 200 yards

❷ MANOR FARM Egerton SY14 8AW (01829 720261)   £25.00 - £30.00 🛏3d1t all en suite ♦♦♦♦   Tourist Information Centre listed 🍴 24 hours notice   🚲   Open all year ★ ★ ★ ★ self catering cottage accommodation also available 🚶About 1.5 miles

❸ HAYCROFT FARM BED & BREAKFAST Peckforton Hall Lane Spurstow CW6 9TF (01829 260389) 💻www.haycroftfarm.co.uk   £22.50 to £27.50 with private or en suite bathroom   🛏2d2t1f1d/t   ♦♦♦♦   Tourist Information Centre listed   🍴no but good pub within walking distance (half a mile) 🍴£5.00 week notice   ⬜drying room ⬜dryer and washer   🚲 Bike washing available   🚌   Open all year   Very close to A49 but very quiet, secluded location   🚶2.25 miles

❹ NEWTON HALL Newton Lane Tattenhall CH3 9NE   (01829 770153)   £30.00 🛏1f1d1s ♦♦♦♦   Tourist Information Centre listed 🍴 with confirmation ⬜heated in winter   🚲 Bike washing hose   🚌   🚶About one mile

❺ HIGHER HUXLEY HALL Red Lane Huxley CH3 9BZ (01829 781484) 💻info@huxleyhall.co.uk   £45.00   🛏2t/d2d/3s   ♦♦♦♦silver award   Tourist Information Centre listed 🍴dinner with advance notification £30.00 🍴with advance notification £7.00, no charge for bottle filling ⬜drying room sometimes available Towel rails in rooms and central heating in winter ⬜available to guests staying 2 nights or more, notice needed 🚲 🔧 Pressure hose for bike washing 🚌 for groups possibly Open most of the year 🚶next to the route

❻ CARRIAGES New Russia Hall Chester Road Gateseath Tattenhall CH3 9AH (01829 770958) £25.00 🛏3f1d ♦♦♦   Tourist Information Centre listed 🍴£3.00 ⬜radiators Cycle storage available Open 365 days   Public house 🚶2 miles

❼ THE CHESHIRE CAT Whitchurch Road Christleton Chester CH3 6AE (01244 332200) 💻www.innkeeperslodge.com (chester south east) Price per room is £55.00 midweek and £58.00 weekends   🛏14 rooms   ♦♦♦   Tourist Information Centre listed 🍴meals available all day 7.00am - 10.00pm 🍴 ⬜ 🚲 🔧 Hose for bike washing 🚌   Open all year 🚶near the route on the A41

❽ RAMADA CHESTER Whitchurch Road Chester CH3 5QL (01244 332121) 💻www.ramadachester.co.uk   £40.00 - £70.00   🛏126fdt   ★ ★ ★ ★   Tourist Informa-tion Centre listed 🍴24 hour room service, brasserie style restaurant, bar food 🍴£8.00 notice 8 hours   🚲   Hose for bike washing Open all year   Leisure club on site includes indoor pool, sauna, steam room, gymnasiums and solarium(chargeable) and is complimen-tary for guests   🚶near the route - located on the A41, south of Chester at Christleton

❾ LABURNUM HOUSE   2 St Annes Street Chester CH1 3HS   (01244 380313) 💻www.laburnumhousechester.co.uk   £28.00   🛏1s2t/d2d1f all en suite TV and tea and coffee making facilities and central heating   ♦♦♦   Tourist Information Centre listed   🍴 ⬜ radiators, also outhouse can be heated on request for clothes drying   ⬜ washing machine available with dryer   🚲 🔧 Cycle washing facilities and space to work on bikes   Warm, friendly hospitality Open all year 🚶0.2 miles Two minutes walk from the nearest exit off the cycle route, Cow Lane Bridge, and four minutes walk from the city centre

Hostels and Campsites

MALPAS TO CHESTER

① MANOR WOOD COUNTRY CARAVAN PARK Manor Wood Coddington CH3 9EN (01829 782990) 💻www.cheshire-caravan-sites.co.uk Λ £15.00 - £20.00 per night ★★★★ Tourist Information Centre listed ⊺tumble dryer ⊡washing machine Hose available for bike washing Caravan touring site also Open all year 🚴1.75 miles

② HAYCROFT FARM BED AND BREAKFAST AND CAMPING AND CARAVAN SITE Peckforton Hall lane Spurstow Tarporley CW6 9TF (01829 260389) 💻www.haycroftfarm.co.uk Λ12 Sites also available for caravans Very close to A49 but very quiet, secluded location 🚴2.25 mile

③ SHADY OAK PUB Bear Beeston Castle Food Λ£2.50 per tent Showers £1 Electricity £2.50 🚴On the route

④ BRICKFIELD FARM 2 High Street Tarporley CW6 0EA (01829 732738) Λ Water Toilet Open all year 🚴2.25 miles

⑤ CARRIAGES New Russia Hall Chester Road Gatesheath Tattenhall CH3 9AH (01829 770958) Λ7 🚴2 miles

⑥ NETHERWOOD TOURING SITE Whitchurch Road Christleton CH3 6AF (01244 335583) 💻www.netherwoodtouringsite.co.uk Λ4 £10.00 - £13.00 Tourist Information Centre listed Open March 1st to October 31st Price includes hot water, showers, hair dryer and shaving point Advance booking essential 🚴alongside the route

⑦ BIRCH BANK FARM Stamford Lane Christleton CH3 7QD (01244 335233) 💻www.birchbankfarm.co.uk Λ10 Tent £4.00 plus £2.00 per adult, £1.00 per child Small caravan / camping site on working farm Free of traffic noise Good showers and toilets Open1st May to 31st October 🚴one mile

⑧ THORNLEIGH PARK FARM Ferry Lane Higher Ferry Chester CH1 6QF (01244 371718) 💻siddfam@aol.com Λ5 £3.50 per adult per night Children (under 16) £2.00 per night Listed with Chester TIC for camping Toilets and showers available Open all year 🚴About 2 miles Also 0.75 miles from River Dee cycletrack and 1 mile from Chester-Connahs Quay cycletrack

⑨ CHESTER BACKPACKERS 67 Boughton Chester CH3 5AF (01244 400185) 💻www.chesterbackpackers.com £13.00 in dormitory, £18.50 single and £34.00 per twin or double room ⟍1x18 bed dormitory, 1x 8 bed and 1d/s and 3t/s ★★ Tourist Information Centre listed 🔴self catering ⊺tumble dryer and radiators ⊡ 🚲 Open 365 days 🚴100 metres, exit south from the canal towpath, east of Chester centre

⑩ YHA CHESTER 40 Hough Green Chester CH4 8JD (01244 680056) 💻www.yha.org.uk £17.50 members £20.50 non-members ⟍100 beds in total in rooms of 2 to 10 beds ★★ Tourist Information Centre listed 🔴price includes breakfast Evening meals available for pre-booked groups of 10 or more (£5.50) Self-catering kitchen available 🔴order in advance by 9.00 night before ⊺drying room only heated in winter ⊡coin-op washer and coin-op dryer Cycle store Open all year 🚴1.25 miles

63

Food and Drink Suggestions

Note: The listings below are not comprehensive.
See red symbols on maps for the location of even more cafes (🍽️) and pubs (🅿️)

THE COCK O'BARTON INN Barton Village Barton Road (A534) SY14 7HU (01829 782277) 💻www.thecockobarton.com Traditional to gastro, including snacks, sandwiches, full meals, vegetarian and specials Full menu and specials available 12.30 - 2.30 and 5.30 - 9.00 Monday to Saturday with a breakfast menu Sunday 10.30 - 12.00 and full menu and Sunday lunch 12.00 - 8.00 Sunday Full meal and drink in the £5.00 - £10.00 range Places available where bikes can be secured with own lock Parties of cyclists welcome 🚲 located just off the A534, about 0.75 miles north of Stretton

THE BICKERTON POACHER Wrexham Road Malpas SY14 8BE (01829 720226) English and European menu served 12.00 - 2.30 and 5.00 - 9.00 Price range for a full meal and drink £5.00 - £10.00 with two course OAP specials at £4.95 🚲 🚲one mile

THE COPPERMINE Nantwich Road Broxton CH3 9JH (01829 782293) Sandwiches and snacks, vegetarian, senior citizens' menu, a la carte and specials,ribs, duck etc. , home-made burgers Open 12.00 - 3.00 and 6.00 - 11.00 with food served 12.00 - 2.00 and 6.30 - 8.00 Price range from under £5.00 to over £10.00 Picturesque setting with large garden / patio area 🚲one mile

BURWARDSLEY VILLAGE STORE AND POST OFFICE Harthill Road Burwardsley CH3 9NU (01829 770359) 💻mandy_geall@hotmail.com Cold snacks, drinks and confectionery Picnic area next to car park Outside toilet for use on request Open 8.00am - 1.00pm from Monday to Saturday, also 2.00pm - 7.30pm Wednesday and Saturday and 8.30am - 12.00 midday Sunday 🚲on the route

CHESHIRE WORKSHOPS - see visitor attractions for details

SHADY OAK PUB Bear Beeston Castle Food 🚲On the route

STUART'S TABLE AT THE FARMERS ARMS Huxley Lane Huxley CH3 9BG (01829 781342) Fresh, healthy food from sandwiches at under £5.00 to full a la carte at over £10.00 No specific children's menu but family dining encouraged Food served 12.00 - 3.00 Tuesday to Friday and 12.00 - 4.00 Saturday and Sunday (closed Monday lunch) and then evenings 6.30 - 9.00 Close more in the winter 🚲 🚲on the route

CHESHIRE FARM ICE CREAM Drumlan Hall Newton Lane Tattenhall CH3 9NE (01829 770446) 💻www.cheshirefarmicecream.co.uk Traditional English snacks Light lunches Afternoon teas Daily Specials Open 7 days a week -see Attractions for details Hot food served 10.00 - 4.00, last orders for cakes and drinks 4.30 Price range for full meal and drink under £5.00 10% discount for cyclists, free second hot drink 🚲1.5 mile

THE PLOUGH INN Plough Lane Christleton CH3 7PT (01244 336096) 💻marphira@aol.com Fresh, home-made, locally-sourced food from sandwiches to a la carte evening meals, vegetarian always available Open all day with lunch served from 12.00 - 3.00 and dinner from 6.30 - 9.00 Price range for lunch is £5.00 - £10.00 and dinner £10.00 plus Cosy traditional pub on one side with superb restaurant with totally fresh and home-produced dishes on the other Popular with cyclists and a useful parking/setting off point for cyclists 🚲 should be available from spring 2006 🚲on the route

THE RING O BELLS Village Road Christleton CH3 7AS (01244 333001) Traditional English meals, sandwiches, snacks, Sunday roasts, vegetarian options Price range for full meal and drink £5.00 - £10.00 Public house opening 11.00 - 11.00 Monday to Saturday and 12.00 - 10.30 Sunday Lunch is served 12.00 - 2.00 Monday to Saturday and 12.00 - 3.00 Sunday with dinner from 6.00 - 9.00 Monday to Saturday and 6.30 - 9.00 Sunday Families welcome in lounge/restaurant Large car park and beer garden with bench seating Patio area overlooking centre of village Post Office opposite pub 🚲Cycle blocks available with padlock hooks 🚲on the route

Tattenhall, just off the route, has some very handy shops

THE OLD TROOPER BEEFEATER Whitchurch Road Christleton CH3 6AE (01244 335784)
Full service modern restaurant Also cosy bar with bar snacks and full meals available Price
range from under £5.00 to over £10.00 Meals provided 12.00noon to 10.00pm Car park
Railings alongside the canal where cycles can be secured Recently refurbished towpath is
part of the Cheshire Cycleway and a 2 - 3 mile ride takes you into the centre of Chester
🚲 on the route

THE FROG AND NIGHTINGALE Canalside Chester CH1 3LH   (01244 347278)
Snacks through to main restaurant menu with vegetarian dishes of the day Full restaurant
menu available from 12.00 - 9.00 daily   Family pub alongside the Shropshire Union Canal
on the edge of the Roman city walls in Chester Selection of real ales, fine wines and
imaginative food   Large outside garden terrace with weekend barbecue all summer   Cycles
can be secured to the chained metal post fence along the perimeter of the canal towpath
🚲 on the route

65

Visitor Attractions

THREAPWOOD on the south western corner of the Cycleway is a fairly spread-out village with a post office and shop There is a windmill tucked away but it is difficult to get a good view of it   SHOCKLACH is small but it has a pub/restaurant and about a mile away is the tiny and picturesque twelfth century church of St. Edith   St Mary's church stands proudly above the road into TILSTON which has a shop and post office and the Carden Arms, not to mention some very comfortable-looking stocks in the centre of the village   Accommodation is available at Tilston Lodge (see under Hotels and Guesthouses)

STRETTON WATERMILL Mill Lane Stretton Nr Farndon SY14 7RS (01606 41331) www.strettonwatermill.org.uk   Step back in time and visit a working mill in beautiful rural Cheshire See one of the country's best preserved demonstration water-powered corn mills Open May to August Tuesday - Sunday and Bank Holiday Mondays 1.00 - 5.00 and weekends only 1.00 - 5.00 during April and September Soft drinks, crisps and cakes on sale   Mill Gift Shop Accessible toilets Attractive picnic area   Small admission charge   cycle racks - bring own lock   on the route

LARKTON HILL (National Trust) has big views and Maiden Castle (half a mile walk from the route), accessible by footpath, an Iron Age fort

The village of HARTHILL has some very attractive buildings and commands fine hilltop views

BURWARDSLEY is a lovely village with a shop and post office and the Pheasant Inn at nearby Higher Burwardsley The PECKFORTON HILLS give a wooded backdrop to the east with Peckforton Castle outlined on the ridge and further north Beeston Castle mounted on its sheer rock cliffs

CHESHIRE WORKSHOPS Burwardsley (01829 770401) Candle-making and other crafts Also restaurant and tearooms   about 0.6 miles

BEESTON CASTLE Beeston (01829 260464) www.english-heritage.org.uk   Dramatic hill-top castle ruins Open daily English Heritage non-members admission charge   500 yards

TATTENHALL is a delight and well worth a look if you like pretty, flower-bedecked pubs and shops and the feel of a busy, lively village   one mile

CHESHIRE FARM ICE CREAM Drumlan Hall Newton Lane Tattenhall CH3 9NE (01829 770446) www.cheshirefarmicecream.co.uk   The largest ice cream parlour in Cheshire with over 30 different flavours of real dairy ice creams and sorbets Tea rooms - see food and drink entry Under 6s play barn Outdoor adventure play area Animal corner Rescued captive bred birds of prey Gift shop Open 7 days 10.00 - 5.30 1st April to 31st October and 10.30 - 5.00 rest of year Closed only Christmas Day, Boxing Day, New Year's Day and a couple of weeks early January - phone for details   Free admission   1.5 miles

TARPORLEY   Good place to take a break if you need services More like a small town than a village - good range of shops and places to eat, a post office, some banks , hotels, public toilets   about 2 miles

CHRISTLETON has a rather fine village pond and the elegant church of St. James The canalside ride into Chester along the Shropshire Union starts just after here

CHESTER is well-known for its remarkable city walls and the Rows - two-tier medieval galleries of shops The river area has a continental feel to it and is a great place to just relax There is plenty to see and do from guided bus or walking tours and a range of river cruises to the museums, galleries, theatres, restaurants etc. CHESTER CATHEDRAL - see www.chestercathedral.com for services and facilities - makes a stunning visit (admission charge) and has a restaurant
The CHESHIRE MILITARY MUSEUM (admission charge) in the castle is open daily and the DEWA ROMAN EXPERIENCE (admission charge), also open daily, has reconstructions and displays   There is horse racing on twelve days of the year at THE ROODEE

GROSVENOR MUSEUM   27 Grosvenor Street Chester CH1 2DD   (01244 402008)
www.grosvenormuseum.co.uk   Discover Chester and its Roman heritage, explore the natural and social history of the area, uncover fine and decorative art. There is an active programme of special exhibitions and events throughout the year   Open all year Monday - Saturday 10.30 - 5.00 and Sunday 1.00 - 4.00 Admission free   0.5 miles

Even if you don't stop for any of this, the canalside ride into and through the city is full of canal-type interest - Northgate locks for example - three staircase locks cut out of rock town centre about 500 yards from the route along the canal.

See map on page 12 for more detail on Chester's array of attractions.

There are some quiet lanes near Beeston, despite the area being popular with visitors

The Pheasant Inn at Higher Burwardsley, near the route.
Good grub and splendid views from the Peckforton Hills

Bike Shops

The Bike Factory 153-161 Boughton Chester CH3 5BH   01244 317893
K Davis 89 Garden Lane Chester CH1 4EW   01244 373408
The Edge Cycleworks 14 Upper Northgate Street Chester CH1 4T   01244 399888
Dave Miller 41 Frodsham Street Chester CH2 3JJ   01244 32606
All the above are within easy striking distance of the route

Tourist Information

Chester TIC   Town Hall Northgate Street Chester CH1 2HJ   01244 402111
www.visitchester.com www.chestercc.gov.uk
Chester Visitor Centre 2 Vicar's Lane Chester CH1 1QX 01244 402111
www.visitchester.com www.chestercc.gov.uk

Family Rides

Most of the following rides follow the line of old railways and their easy gradients are ideal for family cycling. Navigation is very straightforward on these railpath routes and the hardest part is often finding your way onto them as they may be hidden just behind a hedge! The only non-railpath routes are Tatton Park, Delamere Park and the route between Sandbach and Kidsgrove (this actually uses small sections of minor road to link a couple of longer railpath routes and a section of canal towpath). Even these last three examples present easy cycling in a generally traffic-free environment. You can also use the traffic-free sections of day rides 11 (Chester to Connahs Quay, Deeside Path and Chester-Ellesmere Port towpath) and 13 (Northwich and Marbury Country Parks) for shorter traffic-free outings with small children.

Tatton Park - Route Info

Start Free access for cyclists and pedestrians to Tatton Park at the northern and southern gates

Trail Length 8 miles / 13km of estate road and two suggested rides using some tracks, known as the Old Hall Circuit and the Tatton Tour

Trail Condition Wide tarmac estate roads with little traffic on them (there is a charge for motor vehicles to enter the park, so there are generally few cars).

Food & Drink Cafe and restaurant within the stable block complex near The Mansion

Points of Interest There's loads to see without going outside the park boundary. The mere is a great example of landscape gardening and the stable blocks house several shops. The Mansion, gardens, farm and adventure playground are separate, pay-to-enter attractions.

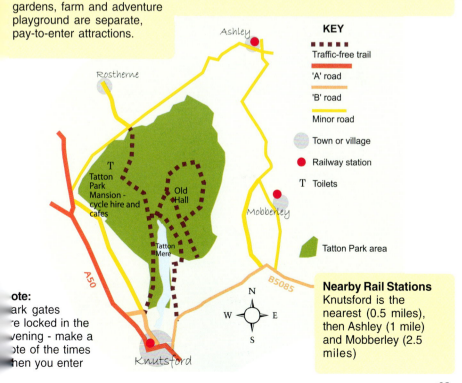

KEY

- Traffic-free trail
- 'A' road
- 'B' road
- Minor road
- Town or village
- Railway station
- T Toilets
- Tatton Park area

Note: ark gates re locked in the vening - make a ote of the times hen you enter

Nearby Rail Stations
Knutsford is the nearest (0.5 miles), then Ashley (1 mile) and Mobberley (2.5 miles)

69

Wirral Way Route Info

From Hooton **To** Near Thurstaston

Trail Length 12 miles / 19km each way

Trail Condition Good hardpacked surface between Hooton and Parkgate but rougher further north, though this is due for improvement

Nearby Rail Stations Hooton is right on the eastern end of the trail and Neston only about a third of mile from the trail where it curves north above the Dee Estuary

Food & Drink Lots of cafes and pubs at Parkgate. Refreshments at Thurstaston Visitor Centre. Also pubs nearby the trail at Willaston and Hooton.

Points of Interest Preserved station south of Willaston (Hadlow Road) and views over the Dee Estuary

KEY

- ▪▪▪▪▪ Traffic-free trail
- ▬▬ 'A' road
- ▬▬ 'B' road
- ⬤ Town or village
- ⬤ Railway station
- T Toilets

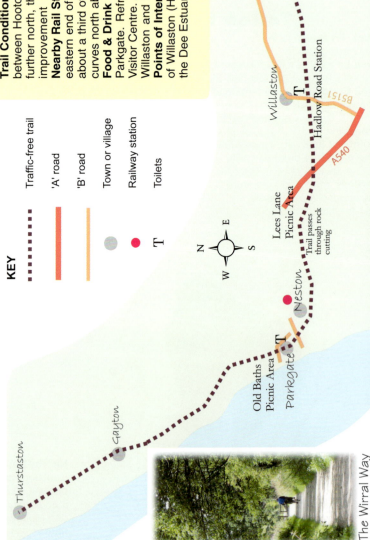

Thurstaston

Gayton

Old Baths
Picnic Area

Parkgate

Neston

Lees Lane
Picnic Area

Trail passes
through rock
cutting

Willaston

Hadlow Road Station

A540

B5151

B5133

Hooton Green

The Wirral Way

70

Whitegate Way Route Info

From Just south of Meadowbank **To** The huge railway bridge by Ravenscough, Cuddington

Trail Length 6 miles / 9.5km each way

Trail Condition OK in good weather but some muddy sections after rain

Nearby Rail Stations Cuddington is just under a mile from the northern end of the trail and Winsford just over 2 miles from the eastern end

Food & Drink Cuddington has a pub but there are no chances for refreshment on the route

Points of Interest The former Whitegate station

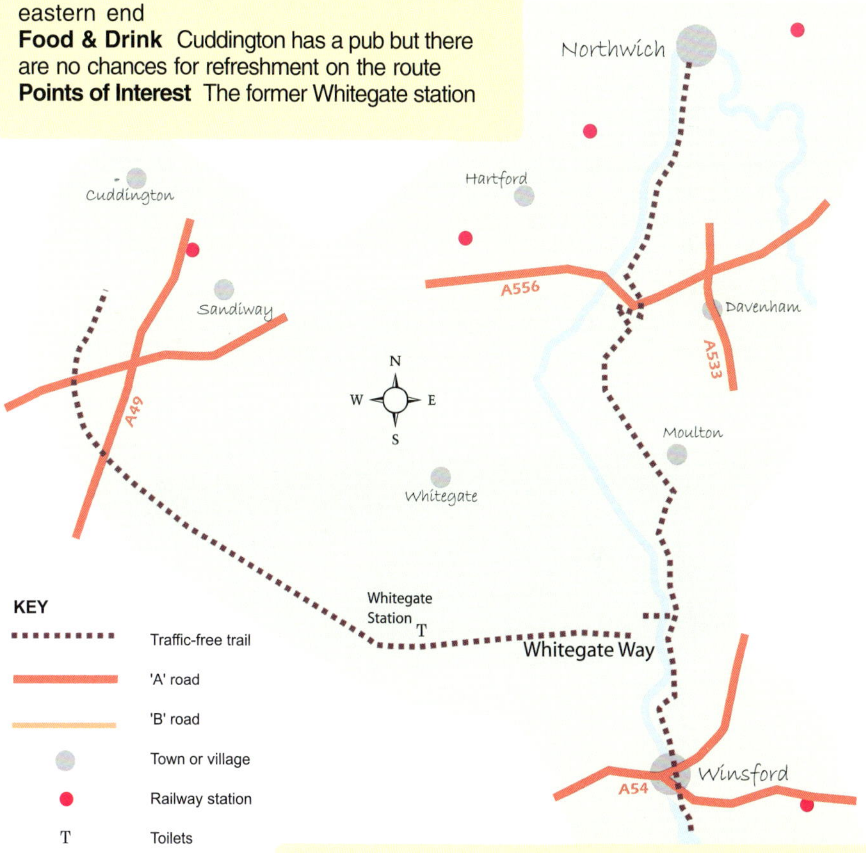

Northwich

Hartford

Cuddington

A556

Sandiway

Davenham

A49

A533

N
W E
S

Moulton

Whitegate

KEY

Whitegate Station T

.... Traffic-free trail

Whitegate Way

——— 'A' road

——— 'B' road

⬤ Town or village

🔴 Railway station

T Toilets

A54   Winsford

Weaver Riverside Route Info
National Cycle Network Route 5

From Rilshaw Meadows Car Park, just south of Winsford   **To** Northwich

Trail Length 5.5 miles / 9km each way

Trail Condition Generally good quality track with the occasional road section. Mainly a riverside path - simply follow NCN 5 signs at junctions

Nearby Rail Stations Winsford (0.5 miles) Greenbank and Northwich stations are both about a mile away

Food & Drink The Red Lion pub is by the route on the Winsford section and there are lots of pubs and eateries in Northwich centre, just a short distance from the northern end of the route

Points of Interest Views over the Weaver Navigation

Delamere Forest Route Info

Start The two circular waymarked trails around Delamere Forest begin at Linmere Lodge visitor centre and both are easily followed using the excellent signs

Trail Length *Whitefield Trail* 7 miles / 11km   *Hunger Hill Trail* 4 miles / 6.5km

Trail Condition Both trails are on wide, well-drained quality forest tracks but you can still expect the odd spot of mud in a forest environment, especially in winter You can also go mountain biking on most of the other main tracks within the forest, though these are not specifically signed as cycle routes and may be a lot muddier than the two waymarked trails (note - not all the tracks within the forest are shown on the map opposite). There is a very detailed map available from Linmere Lodge visitor centre which shows cycling and walking trails and all other tracks in the forest as well as the numerous numbered marker posts - it's well worth the purchase price. There are a few more hills than most of the other family rides but they are still only very moderate ones.

Nearby Rail Stations Delamere train station is right by the main entrance to Delamere Forest on the B5152

Food & Drink Linmere Lodge and Delamere station both have cafes, the latter very popular with cyclists and in a lovely building right next to the platform.

Points of Interest The forest is home to all sorts of plants and animals.

Out on the forest tracks near Linmere Lodge

KEY

- Traffic-free trail
- 'A' road
- 'B' road
- Town or village
- Railway station
- Minor road
- **T** Toilets
- Forest area
- Hunger Hill Trail / Whitefield Trail

Cycle skills area

Hatchmere

Blakemere Moss

T Linmere Lodge

Old Pale

BS152

A54

N
W   E
S

Sandbach to Kidsgrove
Route Info

From Kidsgrove **To** Ettily Heath, Elworth
Trail Length 8.5 miles / 13.5km each way
Trail Condition A mixture of well-surfaced trail and excellently surfaced canal towpath linked by a couple of minor road stretches between the Wheelock Rail Trail, Salt Line and NCN 5 along the Trent & Mersey Canal
Nearby Rail Stations Sandbach (0.75 miles), Alsager (1.25 miles) and Kidsgrove (by the Trent & Mersey canal)
Food & Drink The Romping Donkey pub and Lockside Cafe, both at Hassall Green just off the trail. The Red Bull pub is found on your approach to Kidsgrove, near the junction with the Macclesfield Canal.
Points of Interest Lovely pastoral and canalside scenery. Hassall Green and Sandbach are pretty.

KEY

- ▪▪▪▪ Traffic-free trail
- ▬▬ 'A' road
- ▬▬ 'B' road
- ▬▬ Minor road
- ● Town or village
- ● Railway station

Elworth

Sandbach

A533

A534

Wheelock Rail Trail

B5079

Wheelock

M6

Hassall Green

Hassall

Salt Line

Rode Heath

B5078

Alsager

B5077

Trent & Mersey Towpath

A50

A34

Church Lawton

Kidsgrove

N E S W

Near Lawton Treble Locks,
Trent & Mersey Canal

74

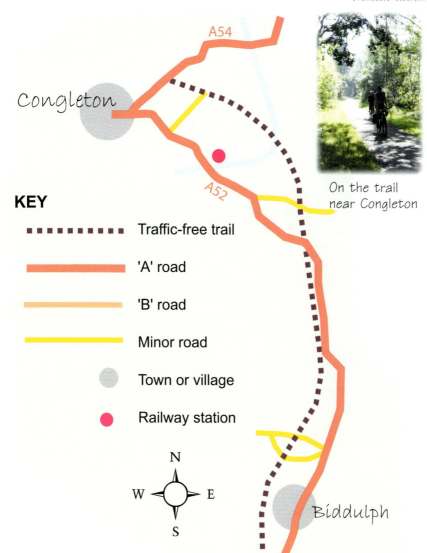

A54

Congleton

A52

On the trail
near Congleton

KEY

▪▪▪▪▪▪▪▪▪ Traffic-free trail

━━━━━ 'A' road

━━━━━ 'B' road

━━━━━ Minor road

● Town or village

● Railway station

N
W ✦ E
S

Biddulph

Biddulph Valley Trail
Route Info

From Congleton, just off the A54 Buxton road, to the north east of the centre
To Newpool Rd, off the A527 at the southern end of Biddulph
Trail Length 5 miles / 8km each way
Trail Condition Decent stone and earth surface
Nearby Rail Stations Congleton (0.5 - 1 miles depending on your route)
Food & Drink Congleton and Biddulph both have plenty of choice
Points of Interest Congleton's attractive town centre. Great views from the trail
over woodland valleys and towards the Peak District

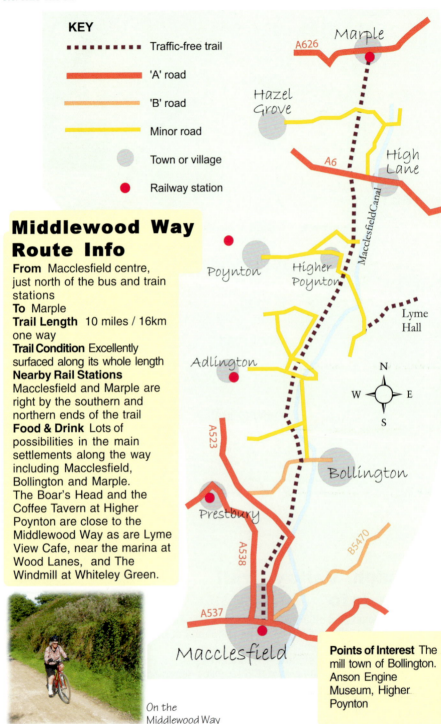

KEY

▪ ▪ ▪ ▪ ▪ ▪ ▪ Traffic-free trail

━━━━ 'A' road

━━━━ 'B' road

━━━━ Minor road

⬤ Town or village

🔴 Railway station

A626

Marple

Hazel Grove

A6

High Lane

Macclesfield Canal

Middlewood Way Route Info

From Macclesfield centre, just north of the bus and train stations
To Marple
Trail Length 10 miles / 16km one way
Trail Condition Excellently surfaced along its whole length
Nearby Rail Stations Macclesfield and Marple are right by the southern and northern ends of the trail
Food & Drink Lots of possibilities in the main settlements along the way including Macclesfield, Bollington and Marple. The Boar's Head and the Coffee Tavern at Higher Poynton are close to the Middlewood Way as are Lyme View Cafe, near the marina at Wood Lanes, and The Windmill at Whiteley Green.

Poynton

Higher Poynton

Lyme Hall

Adlington

N
W · E
S

A523

Bollington

Prestbury

B5470

A538

A537

Macclesfield

On the Middlewood Way

Points of Interest The mill town of Bollington. Anson Engine Museum, Higher Poynton

North of Macclesfield

Route Info

Ridges, Planes and Plains (Medium)
11.5 miles / 18.5km
Off - road   5 miles / 8km
Height Ascended   360m / 1180ft
Suggested Start   Adlington Road car park, Bollington, by the Middlewood Way.
Route Advice   The Middlewood Way is very well-surfaced and flat. The track up to Lyme Park is generally well-surfaced and wide, though can be bumpy and a little muddy in places. Otherwise quiet roads with just a few very steep climbs.
Nearest Train Stations   Prestbury is nearest to the start (about two miles), but Adlington and Poynton are on the same line and Middlewood is on the Buxton line.
Parking   Adlington Road car park, Bollington, by the Middlewood Way.
Food & Drink   Many eateries in Bollington. The Coffee Tavern near Pott Shrigley. Coffee shop,restaurant and an ice cream kiosk at Lyme Park. The Boar's Head and another Coffee Tavern at Higher Poynton are close to the Middlewood Way as are the Lyme View Cafe near the marina at Wood Lanes and the Windmill at Whiteley Green.

Riding the Ridges (Difficult)
19 miles / 30.5km
Off - road   3 miles / 5km
Height Ascended   911m / 2988ft
Suggested Start   Adlington Road car park, Bollington, by the Middlewood Way.
Route Advice   Extreme climbs and fantastic views are the real features of this ride. Up until Disley you are still in the Peak District foothills but beyond the pretty town centre you are transported into a world of contorted Pennine gritstone scenery boasting names like Windgather Rocks and Oldgate Nick. Some of the roads are very minor indeed and steep twisting descents on them require a lot of care and excellent brakes.
Nearest Train Station   Disley station is bang on the route and is on the Manchester-Stockport-Sheffield line.
Parking   Adlington Road car park, Bollington, by the Middlewood Way.
Food & Drink   Many eateries in Bollington. Coffee shop,restaurant and an ice cream kiosk at Lyme Park. Pubs in Kettleshulme and Rainow.

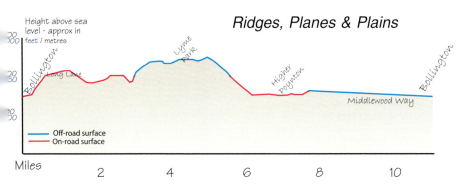

Ridges, Planes & Plains

Along the Way

Ridges, Planes & Plains

Bollington - see pg35 for information.

Long Lane has stunning views- sit and watch the aircraft coming and going at Manchester Airport. Even at this distance they look enormous and seem to be going so slowly they ought to drop out of the sky.

Lyme Park (NT) is a magnificent house with beautiful gardens and much estate land. Some of the roadways are open to cyclists and off-road cycling is available on the 'Knott'. Admission charges to non-NT members for house, garden etc. Grounds open free to cyclists and walkers. 01663 762023 or see www.nationaltrust.org.uk

The Anson Engine Museum on Anson Road in Higher Poynton, about half a mile from the Middlewood Way, has a collection of working order examples of internal combustion engines. Open Fridays, weekends and Bank Holidays from Easter Sunday to the end of October. Programme of special events during the year. Admission charge. Telephone 01625 874426 or see www.enginemuseum.org

The Middlewood Way is an excellent greenway path for cyclists, walkers and horseriders on the site of the former Macclesfield, Bollington and Marple Railway. In places, it runs close to the Macclesfield Canal and its facilities. The old station area at Higher Poynton, the northernmost point of this ride, has picnic tables and is close to a number of refreshment facilities, public toilets, car parking and the Nelson Pit Visitor Centre.

The Macclesfield Canal was completed in 1831 and has been used for leisure since commercial transport ended in the 1960s. There are useful facilities by the canal for Middlewood Way users near Higher Poynton and Wood Lanes.

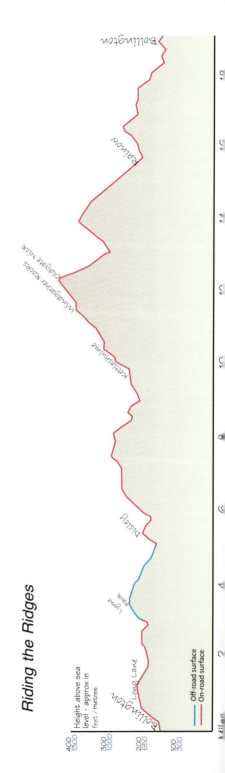

Riding the Ridges

Along the Way

Riding the Ridges

See opposite for information on **Bollington, Long Lane** and **Lyme Park**
Kettleshulme is a small but delightful village boasting the Swan Inn.
Dunge Valley Hidden Gardens are in an unusual Pennine setting, specialising in Himalayan plants. Open March to August. Admission charge. Tearoom.
Open March-August 01663 733787   www.dungevalley.co.uk
Windgather Rocks and Oldgate Nick are both impressive gritstone features of the complex Pennine scenery in the area, with great views. Windgather Rocks are a popular spot for rockclimbers.
Jenkin Chapel A fantastically well-preserved early 18th century building, standing in moorland isolation. Built by voluntary subscription and dedicated to St John the Evangelist.
Kerridge Hill and White Nancy The monument of White Nancy is visible from many points around Bollington and sits on top of the northern end of the striking ridge that is Kerridge Hill. One theory is that it was built to celebrate victory at Waterloo.

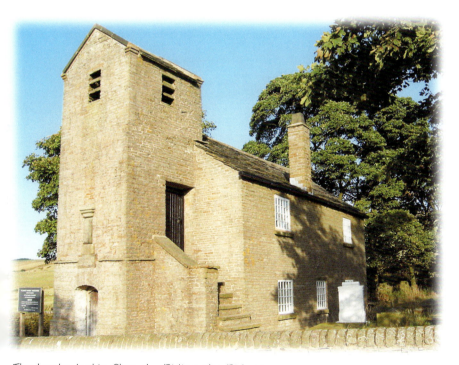

The lovely Jenkin Chapel - Riding the Ridges

79

RIDGES, PLANES & PLAINS

A - B

From Adlington Rd car park
by the Middlewood Way turn
R onto Adlington Rd
then L at the T-junction
by the Dog & Partridge.
Very shortly after
passing under the canal
bridge look for the L
turn by the church onto
the very steep, cobbled
Beeston Brow. Bend L
onto Long Lane
with amazing views
over the Cheshire
Plain. At the
T-junction at
the end of
Long Lane
turn L to
descend.
Take the
next R
signed
Higher
Poynton
and
Coffee
Tavern.
Pass
the
Coffee
Tavern
to come
to a
Methodist
church on your
R. The main
route carries on
on the same road
here as the
Riding the Ridges
ride, or a detour
to Lyme Park heads off
R. For directions on the
detour to Lyme Park see
the start of the Riding the
Ridges ride.

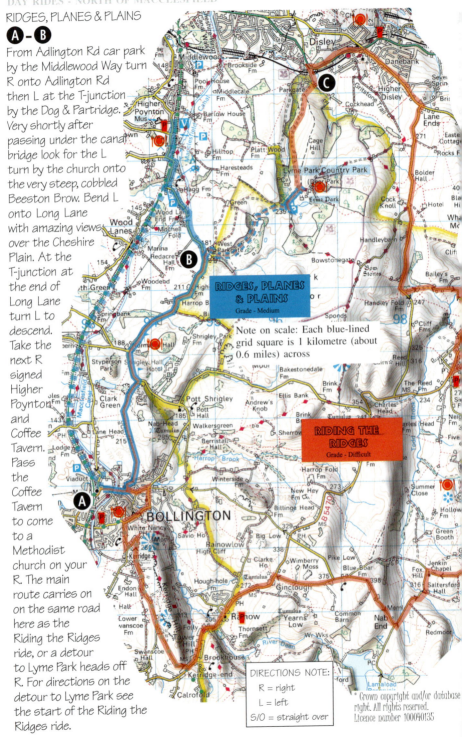

RIDGES, PLANES & PLAINS
Grade - Medium

Note on scale: Each blue-lined
grid square is 1 kilometre (about
0.6 miles) across

RIDING THE RIDGES
Grade - Difficult

DIRECTIONS NOTE:
R = right
L = left
S/O = straight over

© Crown copyright and/or database right. All rights reserved. Licence number 100040135

B - A Having detoured to Lyme Park retrace your steps to the Methodist church and carry on, on the road you turned off, to pass under the Macclesfield Canal and in Poynton pass the car park on the L which is also an access point onto the Middlewood Way. A bridge takes you over the Middlewood Way, then turn first R onto Shrigley Road North, which takes you to the Coffee Tavern (a different one!) and the Boars Head pub. The Anson Engine Museum is next L up Anson Road. To head back along the Middlewood Way retrace your steps to the car park access point and head L onto the trail. It's then just a matter of following this well-surfaced rail trail for about 3.25 miles until you reach the towering and very well-surfaced viaduct above Bollington where you wheel down the stepped ramps to Adlington Rd car park.

RIDING THE RIDGES **B - C**

Follow directions in the Ridges, Planes & Plains ride to the Methodist church at West Parkgate and take the descending track to the R, so as to pass the Methodist church on the R. This will bring you to the lodge entrance to Lyme Park on the R and you enter through the gate here to follow the main track all the way through the woods to emerge at a gate after 0.7 miles (ignore the split R about half way along). Follow the main tarmac track through open grassland to come to the magnificent Lyme Park stately home. Those on a detour from the Ridges, Planes and Plains route can retrace their tracks to the Methodist church past West Parkgate Lodge; if on the Riding the Ridges route pick up the main tarmac exit road out of Lyme Park, past the Cage Hill monument up to the R, all the way to the A6.

C - D

Turn R onto the BUSY & FAST A6. Coming into Disley centre turn R past the White Horse Hotel on the R onto Buxton Old Rd. Climb for 0.8 miles and take the first R onto Mudhurst Lane. Superb views of the Peak's gritstone scenery reveal themselves from this lovely road. Follow the road for around 1.8 miles and on a steep descent take an unsigned L onto a very minor road that descends over a small stream and through woods along a valley bottom. Climb steeply, then past Baileys Farm descend to cross a more major stream before climbing to an unmarked T-junction and R. Follow this minor road to come to a T-junction in Kettleshulme. Go R and pass the Swan Inn. Turn L down the side of the Bulls Head Inn onto a very minor unsigned road and descend past Bent Hall Farm to climb VERY steeply as the road becomes a potholed track, picking up tarmac again to emerge at a T-junction where you go R. At the next crossroads go L, signed Saltersford and Goyt Valley.

D - A

Follow this spectacular 'ridge road' with stunning views for around 1.3 miles to come to a T-junction and turn R, signed Saltersford and Rainow. At the unusual building of Jenkin Chapel bend 90 degrees L and at the next T-junction turn R onto Ewrin Lane, signed Rainow. Just after a phone box turn L onto Smiths Lane, signed Rainow. At the B5470 turn L. Follow it through Rainow, passing the Robin Hood and Rising Sun pubs before turning R down Lidgetts Lane. At the next T-junction turn R and follow the road to Bollington, going R onto Jackson Lane. Follow the Cheshire Cycleway down Chancery Lane, Lord St and Church St to turn L at the mini-roundabout onto the B5090. Descend under the canal then turn R onto Adlington Rd.

South of Alderley Edge

Route Info

From the Past to the Space Age (Medium)
15.5miles / 25km   Off - road 3 miles / 5km
Height Ascended 136m / 446ft
Suggested Start Goostrey
Route Advice Easy going terrain across the Cheshire Plain with a couple of off-road sections that can get muddy after rain but which are generally OK for riding.
Nearest Train Stations Goostrey train station is right by the route start. Chelford station is a couple of miles off the route.
Parking In Goostrey
Food & Drink Spoilt for choice! Goostrey has the Crown and Red Lion pubs and several village shops. The Dog Inn and Ye Olde Parkgate Inn are both at Over Peover. Grasslands Nursery, after Peover Hall, has the very nice Potting Shed Cafe. The Bells of Peover in Little Peover is in a lovely setting. Swan Green has the Crown pub and a well-stocked village store.

Wizards & Elizabethans (Medium)
25 miles / 40 km   Off - road 3 miles / 5km
Height Ascended 450m / 1476ft
Suggested Start Alderley Edge
Route Advice You are in the foothills of the Pennines here and so there are several (usually) shortish but steepish climbs. There are also a few sections of fast A or B road that can be busy but most have the option of pushing down a roadside pavement. This makes this a great adventure route for older children who will enjoy the blend of marvellous scenery, folklore and many ancient buildings they will encounter. Some of the off-road sections can be tricky due to mud or cobbles but again these are generally short and will only add to the adventure. If you ride this route outside of the rush hour you will be mainly on quiet roads and reasonably surfaced off-road tracks.
Nearest Train Station Alderley Edge
Parking In Alderley Edge and at the southern end of Redesmere, near Siddington
Food & Drink Lots of nice eateries in Alderley Edge. For Henbury see page 33.

Wizards & Elizabethans

From the Past to the Space Age takes you to the awe-inspiring Jodrell Bank

From the Past to the Space Age

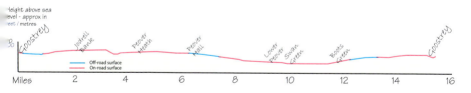

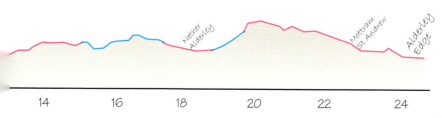

FROM THE PAST TO THE SPACE AGE

A - B   From Goostrey centre head east, past the church and Red Lion pub, and very shortly go L up the track signed Public Path to Blackden Heath and Jodrell Bank. (If starting from Goostrey station go R out of the station and next R up this track.) The track passes through buildings at Blackden Hall and continues to meet a road where you turn R. Very shortly turn L onto an unsigned road and R at the next crossroads, again unmarked, with great views of Jodrell Bank radio telescope on this section. Bend 90 degrees R to cross over the railway to come to the Jodrell Bank visitor centre (a 'must' if you haven't been - see Along the Way). Take the next L, signed Over Peover, onto Batemill Lane. Dip past Bate Mill and climb under the railway to meet a crossroads and go R. Just past Snelson Lane on the R turn L onto Well Bank Lane, signed Over Peover. In Over Peover (marked Peover Heath on the Ordnance Survey map) pass the pretty Dog Inn.

After the Dog Inn continue to a crossroads and S/O to continue through Over Peover past Ye Olde Parkgate Inn. On the edge of the village turn L onto Grotto Lane signed Goostrey & Congleton. At the next crossroads turn R, signed Over Peover Church/Hall & Goostrey. Shortly turn R onto the bridleway that is the main entrance to Peover Hall. Past the entrance to Peover Hall and church on the R (footpath access only) continue to the gate where the track becomes a narrower grassy track - still a decent surface in the dry. This eventually turns to tarmac past large greenhouses to meet the A50.

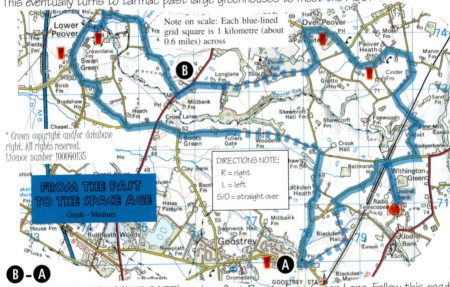

Note on scale: Each blue-lined grid square is 1 kilometre (about 0.6 miles) across

° Crown copyright and/or database right. All rights reserved.
Licence number 100040135

FROM THE PAST TO THE SPACE AGE
Grade - Medium

DIRECTIONS NOTE:
R = right
L = left
S/O = straight over

B - A   Turn L onto the A50 (TAKE CARE) and go first R onto Free Green Lane. Follow this road for about 1.3 miles to take the third L turn, by the Millennium seat. Now in Lower Peover turn L onto Barrows Brow (leading to Church Walk). Follow the main track to the lovely Bells of Peover pub. Through the car park turn R onto the cobbled lane and at the end of The Cobbles go L onto the B5081. Just through Swan Green take the first L onto Foxcovert Lane and next R onto a very minor road. L at the end of this road then bear L onto Townfield Lane at its junction with Heath Lane and Sandy Lane (pass the brick farm buildings on the R). At the A50 head S/O onto Booth Bed Lane. Very shortly turn L, a 'No Through Rd' onto Boots Green. Follow this lane as it becomes a stony track before narrowing further, to follow a sign for Blackden Heath, Jodrell Bank, Peover Church. This grassy single track passes through trees and emerges at a road. Turn R and continue R at every opportunity to get back to Goostrey.

WIZARDS AND ELIZABETHANS

A - B From Alderley Edge high street (London Road) head south to the roundabout with the B5087 and go L up Chapel Road. Follow for around 2 miles to come into Mottram St Andrew. Turn R here onto Oak Road. At the end of Oak Road go R and immediate L to follow the Cheshire Cycleway short cut route. Go R and L onto Birtles Lane by the Black Greyhound Smithy. Go next L signed Henbury and Broken Cross and continue to the T-junction with Whirley Lane and go L then R onto Andertons Lane. In Henbury go R onto Pepper Street and S/O the A537. Follow School Lane for 1.4 miles to turn L onto Fanshawe Lane.

WIZARDS AND ELIZABETHANS
Grade - Medium

DIRECTIONS NOTE:
R = right
L = left
S/O = straight over

C - A Pass Birtles Hall and very shortly after the church turn L up the well-surfaced and signed bridleway. Pass between the first group of buildings and pick up the earth track that improves past Harmans Barn to come to a T-junction. L here onto a cobbled lane and follow the track past some very desirable residences to enter woods. The route goes R at the next junction of Hocker Lane and Bradford Lane, but you can visit the spectacular Nether Alderley Mill and Church by bearing L on Bradford Lane to the A34 and going L. Back on the main route bear L at a split to follow the rubble track that climbs steeply past the Wizard Caravan Park. At the T-junction with Finlow Hill Lane go R and continue to the B5087 and R here to crossroads and L onto School Lane. Carry on this road to pass National Trust Hare Hill Gardens entrance. Take the next L onto Oak Road, signed Mottram St Andrew and retrace your outward route.

B - C In about 1 mile go R (still on Fanshawe Lane), signed dead end and bridleway. At the gates to Old Fanshawe Vicarage go L onto the cinder path which passes Redesmere and continue on a wider track to the A34 and turn L WITH CARE. Go first R down Mill Lane. Pass round the back of Capesthorne and follow the road to an unsigned T-junction to go L. Stay on Chelford Road to come into Siddington where you meet a T-junction and go L, signed Macclesfield (now on the B5392). Turn L onto the A34 and second R back onto Redesmere Lane. Follow the road for about 1.75 miles to turn L opposite a small row of brick houses. Climb on this road and in about 1 mile go S/O the A537 onto Birtles Lane.

Along the Way

From the Past to the Space Age

Goostrey seems pretty popular with cyclists.

Jodrell Bank is well worth the modest admission price just to walk right up to the enormous radio telescope dish and marvel at the scale. There are interesting exhibits and a shop and cafe and there is also a 35 acre arboretum.

The Dog Inn at Peover Heath is an old and interesting building, originally cottages and becoming a pub in the mid-nineteenth century. Real ales, food, accommodation. 01625 861421. **Peover Hall** is an Elizabethan manor house with gardens and landscaped park and was headquarters to General Patton during part of World War 2. Opening details from 01565 632358. See also nearby **St. Lawrence's Church.** Further on, at Lower Peover, **The Bells of Peover** public house (01565 722269), ancient enough itself, was a meeting place for Patton and Eisenhower. Also at Lower Peover see the picturesque half timbered **St.Oswald's Church.**

Wizards and Elizabethans

For Alderley Edge, Hare Hill parkland and gardens, Capesthorne Hall and Nether Alderley Mill see Chapter 2.

Henbury Hall and garden are not open to the casual or individual visitor.

The southern end of the ride takes you past the tranquil and beautiful **Redesmere**, a popular duck feeding spot, offering the possibility of seeing herons, buzzards and a variety of wildfowl.

Nether Alderley Mill and the nearby church are beautiful and unusual buildings and well worth the short detour off the main route.

There are great views over the Peak hills from **Finlow Hill Lane** towards the end of the ride.

Woodland bridleway track at Peover Hall,
From the Past to the Space Age ride

No Through Road - but not for cyclists; at Boots Green riding From the Past to the Space Age

Around Congleton

Route Info

Around the Dane (Medium)
16 miles / 26 km
Off - road 1 mile / 1.6 km
Height Ascended 224m / 735ft
Suggested Start Congleton centre
Route Advice Reasonably quiet country lanes are the norm on this rolling ride, but there's a lovely bridleway section at Davenport Hall.
Nearest Train Stations Congleton is almost on the route. Holmes Chapel is a couple of miles away from the Brereton Heath to Swettenham stretch, Goostrey a bit further.
Parking In and around Congleton.
Food & Drink Plenty of places in Congleton. There are places on the way - the Brownlow Inn at Brownlow and the Blue Bell Inn at Spen Green. The highlight though is the Swettenham Arms, simply for its beautiful setting.

Castle Folly? (Difficult)
13 miles / 20.5km
Off - road 4 miles / 6.5km
Height Ascended 406m / 1332ft
Suggested Start Congleton centre
Route Advice Most of this ride is actually easy riding on quiet roads and the traffic-free Biddulph Valley Way. However, the climb up to Mow Cop is extended and, in places, very steep - but worth it for the incredible views and a chance to visit the unusual Mow Cop Castle.
Nearest Train Station Congleton station is almost on the route.
Parking In and around Congleton.
Food & Drink Plenty of places in Congleton. The Congleton Garden Centre Tearoom and the Horseshoe Inn come early on in the ride. Mow Cop has The Cheshire View Inn and there is the Staffordshire Knot at Gillow Heath near where you join the Biddulph Valley Way.

Biddulph Valley Way - Castle Folly?

Gothic splendour at Astbury -
Around the Dane

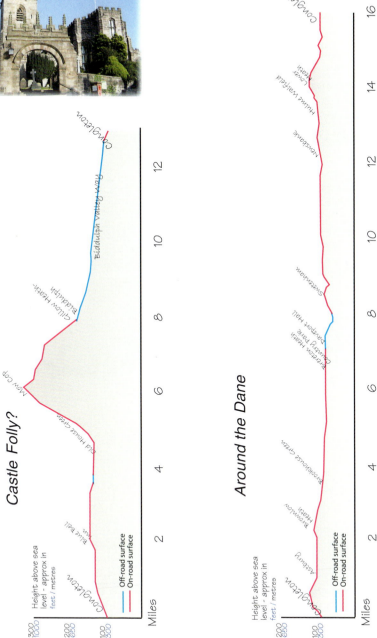

Castle Folly?

Height above sea
level - approx in
feet / metres

300 / 1000
200 / 650
100 / 300

Congleton

Miles

Blue Bell Inn

Old House Green

Mow Cop

Gillow Heath - Biddulph

Biddulph Valley Way

Congleton

Off-road surface
On-road surface

2   4   6   8   10   12

Around the Dane

Height above sea
level - approx in
feet / metres

200 / 650
100 / 300

Congleton

Miles

Astbury

Brownlow

Brownlow Heath

Brookhouse Green

Brereton Heath
Country Park

Davenport Hall

Swettenham

Newsbank

Hulme Walfield

Lower Heath

Congleton

Off-road surface
On-road surface

2   4   6   8   10   12   14   16

89

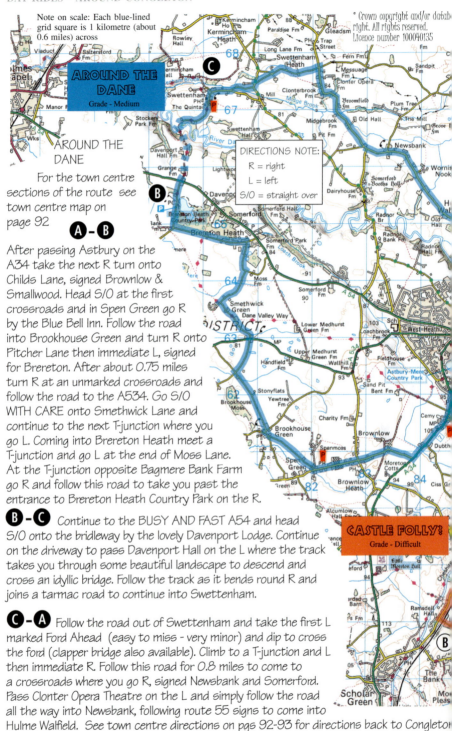

Note on scale: Each blue-lined grid square is 1 kilometre (about 0.6 miles) across

° Crown copyright and/or datab right. All rights reserved. Licence number 100040135

AROUND THE DANE
Grade - Medium

DIRECTIONS NOTE:
R = right
L = left
S/O = straight over

AROUND THE DANE

For the town centre sections of the route see town centre map on page 92

A - B

After passing Astbury on the A34 take the next R turn onto Childs Lane, signed Brownlow & Smallwood. Head S/O at the first crossroads and in Spen Green go R by the Blue Bell Inn. Follow the road into Brookhouse Green and turn R onto Pitcher Lane then immediate L, signed for Brereton. After about 0.75 miles turn R at an unmarked crossroads and follow the road to the A534. Go S/O WITH CARE onto Smethwick Lane and continue to the next T-junction where you go L. Coming into Brereton Heath meet a T-junction and go L at the end of Moss Lane. At the T-junction opposite Bagmere Bank Farm go R and follow this road to take you past the entrance to Brereton Heath Country Park on the R.

B - C Continue to the BUSY AND FAST A54 and head S/O onto the bridleway by the lovely Davenport Lodge. Continue on the driveway to pass Davenport Hall on the L where the track takes you through some beautiful landscape to descend and cross an idyllic bridge. Follow the track as it bends round R and joins a tarmac road to continue into Swettenham.

CASTLE FOLLY?
Grade - Difficult

C - A Follow the road out of Swettenham and take the first L marked Ford Ahead (easy to miss - very minor) and dip to cross the ford (clapper bridge also available). Climb to a T-junction and L then immediate R. Follow this road for 0.8 miles to come to a crossroads where you go R, signed Newsbank and Somerford. Pass Clonter Opera Theatre on the L and simply follow the road all the way into Newsbank, following route 55 signs to come into Hulme Walfield. See town centre directions on pgs 92-93 for directions back to Congleton

CASTLE FOLLY?

For the town centre sections of the route see town centre map overleaf.

A - B Follow Moss Road past Congleton Garden Centre (with tearooms) to take the next L turn before the rail bridge. Parallel the railway then head away from it to bear L onto Mow Lane. Turn R by the Horseshoe Inn onto Fence Lane. Bend 90 degrees L to ignore the next R, following Scholar Green signs. Ignore Oak Lane on the R as Fence Lane becomes Wharf Lane. As Wharf Lane rises, just before crossing the railway, branch off L, signed as a dead end. Follow this road to the railway and use the underpass on your L to go under the railway. Emerge at a T-junction to go L, leaving the hamlet of Ackers Crossing on Station Rd. Pass the beautiful buildings at Old House Green and turn L up Drumber Lane, signed Mow Cop, to pass over the railway on a level crossing.

B - C Climbing towards the outline of Mow Cop Castle, take the first R down Birch Tree Lane, signed Mount Pleasant. At the next T-junction turn L onto Mount Pleasant Rd. Climb into Mount Pleasant and just past the Post Office turn L up Clare St and bend R onto Church St. Climbing VERY STEEPLY now, pass Woodcock Primary School and bear R onto Woodcock Lane. In Mow Cop go R by the chapel building to immediately pass the village shop / post office. Go L onto High St which will lead you past the spectacular Mow Cop Castle.

C - A After exploring the views carry on to the T-junction with Wood St. and turn R passing radio masts and descend steeply to a T-junction by the Mow Cop Inn and L. Admire the lofty views from this ridge road and take the next R turn onto Mow Lane. This descends steeply and coming into the Gillow Heath area of Biddulph look for the L turn onto Well Lane. Follow this until it bends R to cross the Biddulph Valley Way traffic free trail. Go L onto the trail and pass through Whitemoor Local Nature Reserve. Continue on past the sign welcoming you to Cheshire.

For directions from the Biddulph Valley Way back to Congleton see overleaf.

Routes Into Congleton

DIRECTIONS NOTE:
R = right
L = left
S/O = straight over

AROUND THE DANE

STARTING IN THE TOWN CENTRE

With the Tourist Information Centre behind you and on your R head down High St and onto Bridge St then Duke St (dismount and push on the pedestrianised section). Turn L onto Swan Bank and L in front of the Lion & Swan Hotel onto Wagg St. Follow this road round as it becomes Waggs Rd and eventually Fol Hollow. This meets the A34 where you go L (CARE NEEDED - BUSY & FAST). On the A34 pass the village of Astbury off to your L (worth a visit for its beautiful church and pub - see Along the Way).

STARTING AT THE TRAIN STATION

Turn L onto the main road in front of the station to cross the railway bridge and immediate R onto Cross Lane. At the end of Cross Lane go R onto Leek Rd and follow along Canal Rd, Canal St and Albert Place to the tourist office then use the 'Starting in the Town Centre' directions.

FINISHING IN THE TOWN CENTRE

Continue through Hulme Walfield into Congleton and take the second L onto Lower Heath Avenue, continuing on NCN route 55. Meet the A34 at a VERY BUSY INTERSECTION and cross to the opposite side of the road past the Grove Inn. Head L on the pavement cycle lane and turn R onto Jackson Road. Follow this road to bend right, between river and industrial estate, onto Riverdane Rd. Continue on to parallel the line of the river, into Congleton Park, crossing the bridge on your left and heading up the path to the busy A54. Jink L then R across this road onto Herbert St and follow in a straight line to turn R onto Bromley Rd. Follow Bromley Rd all the way to the traffic lights at the A527 and dismount to cross it and push down the one way road that is Lawton St. This will take you back to the Town Hall on High St.

FINISHING AT THE TRAIN STATION

As for the finish in the town centre but then at the Town Hall head down Albert Place, which becomes Canal St. then Canal Rd. Over the railway bridge take the first L onto Cross Lane. Follow this to the A527 and jink L then R, with care, across this fast road to the station.

CASTLE FOLLY?

STARTING AT THE TRAIN STATION

Turn L onto the main road in front of the station to cross the railway bridge and immediate R onto Cross Lane. At the end of Cross Lane go R and first L, before the rail bridge, onto Moss Road.

STARTING IN THE TOWN CENTRE

From the tourist information office in the Town Hall head across the High St and down Albert Place, which becomes Canal St. then Canal Rd. Just over the railway bridge turn R onto Moss Rd.

FINISHING AT THE TRAIN STATION

Cross over the A527 near the Welcome to Cheshire sign and exit at the next bridge, going down the large earth steps on your L and L onto Reades Lane. Over Biddulph Brook climb to the A527 and head S/O onto Leek Road. After just less than half a mile turn R back onto Cross Lane and retrace your outward route to the station.

FINISHING IN THE TOWN CENTRE

After passing the Welcome to Cheshire sign simply continue on the Biddulph Valley Way for around 3 miles to pass under the railway. Take the next cycle exit on the L just before a bridge and head L onto Bromley Rd through a housing estate. Follow Bromley Rd all the way to the traffic lights at the A527 and dismount to cross it and push down the one way road that is Lawton St. This will take you back to the Town Hall on High St.

Along the Way

Around the Dane

Congleton - see Chapter 4.

Astbury is small but well worth a stop to see **St. Mary's Church** and if it's not too early in the ride, enjoy a visit to the **Egerton Arms** - food, drink (and accommodation) and interesting old music hall or theatre posters. **Astbury Mere Country Park** (see Chapter 4) is not far away.

Further along the ride, **Brereton Heath Country Park** has a 15 acre lake and much woodland - public toilets also.

Swettenham is a delightful village with the Swettenham Arms making a great place for a break. **The Quinta Arboretum** here was established by Sir Bernard Lovell and there are wild flower meadows above the brook. **St. Peter's Church** is reportedly linked to the Swettenham Arms by a tunnel.

A mile or two past Swettenham is **The Clonter Opera Theatre**, quite a surprising thing to chance upon in rural Cheshire.

The beautiful bridleway section through Davenport Hall - Around the Dane

Your high point at Mow Cop Castle on the Castle Folly? ride

Castle Folly?

Congleton - see Chapter 4.

There are some eye-catching across-country views of **Mow Cop Castle** before you cross the railway to head up into **Mow Cop**, a small village but with much of interest. The Chapel Museum is a restored Wesleyan chapel with an exhibition on the turbulent religious and industrial history of Mow Cop - tel 01782 522004.

The castle was built in 1754, largely as it is today, as a landscape feature cum summerhouse and the views over both Cheshire and Staffordshire from the castle are stunning. Huge outdoor meetings of the Primitive Methodists took place in the area in both the nineteenth and twentieth centuries.

The **Old Man of Mow** is an impressive 65 feet high rock edifice with a number of explanations as to its being. The village has a shop/post office and the Cheshire View Inn.

The **Biddulph Valley Way** back into Congleton is a former railway line now open for walkers, cyclists and horseriders.

The Biddulph Valley Way at Congleton

South of Sandbach

Route Info

Crosses & Canals (Easy)
15 miles / 24 km
Off - road   6.5miles / 10.5 km
Height Ascended 230m / 753ft
Suggested Start Sandbach Town Hall.
Route Advice A mixture of roads and some very high quality traffic free trail, including the Trent & Mersey towpath (resurfaced as part of National Cycle Network route 5), the Salt Line and the Wheelock Rail Trail. You'll have to mix with some town traffic around Sandbach but this is only a small proportion of the ride and the majority of roads are pretty quiet.
Nearest Train Station Sandbach station is actually 1.3 miles east of Sandbach centre, along the A533, in Elworth.
Parking Plenty of parking in Sandbach.
Food & Drink The beautifully located Lock 57 cafe is at Hassall Green. Pubs include the Romping Donkey at Hassall Green, The Horseshoe at Lawton Heath End and the Red Bull at the end of the towpath ride, near Kidsgrove. Plenty of places in Sandbach as you would expect.

The Trent & Mersey Canal near Hassall Green

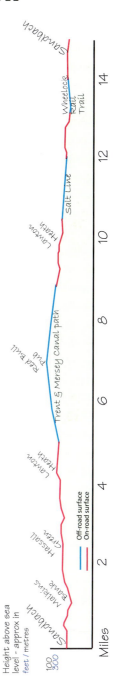

CROSSES & CANALS

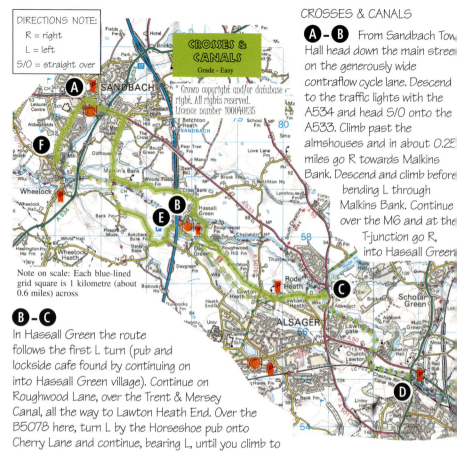

© Crown copyright and/or database right. All rights reserved. Licence number 100040135

Note on scale: Each blue-lined grid square is 1 kilometre (about 0.6 miles) across

A - B From Sandbach Town Hall head down the main street on the generously wide contraflow cycle lane. Descend to the traffic lights with the A534 and head S/O onto the A533. Climb past the almshouses and in about 0.25 miles go R towards Malkins Bank. Descend and climb before bending L through Malkins Bank. Continue over the M6 and at the T-junction go R, into Hassall Green

B - C

In Hassall Green the route follows the first L turn (pub and lockside cafe found by continuing on into Hassall Green village). Continue on Roughwood Lane, over the Trent & Mersey Canal, all the way to Lawton Heath End. Over the B5078 here, turn L by the Horseshoe pub onto Cherry Lane and continue, bearing L, until you climb to the road bridge over the Trent & Mersey Canal. Don't cross the bridge but turn R onto the canal towpath, keeping the canal on your L.

C - D

Follow the canal towpath as it passes under the A50 and then ascends alongside the lovely Lawton Treble Locks, with views of Mow Cop Castle folly in the distance. Use the bridge to keep on the towpath (canal now on your R) and continue on through lovely open countryside, under the A50 near Church Lawton, and in about 1.3 miles pass the Red Bull flight of locks to emerge at the A34. This is the end of your outward route and a good opportunity to break at the Red Bull pub just across the road.

D - E

Retrace your route along the canal towpath back to the road bridge you joined at and keep following your outward route to arrive at the T-junction by the Horseshoe Inn. Turn R and barely 0.25 miles bear L onto the B5078 and descend before joining the Salt Line (access point has Salt Line sign so you can't really miss it). Follow this decent quality trail for 1.5 miles, crossing a lane and going under the M6 to emerge at a road opposite the Salt Line car park.

E - F

Turn L here, at the end of the Salt Line and climb sharply to take the next R turn (Mill Lane), towards Wheelock. Follow this road until the track on your R which you take, past a small row of houses (Jubilee Villas), opposite a L turn which is actually a dead end to Bank Farm. Follow the track across the golf course and climb towards the Trent & Mersey Canal to pick up a bridleway track on your L (you are now following the canal on your R). This track joins the Wheelock Rail Trail to cross the Trent and Mersey Canal and meet the A534 (CROSS WITH CARE).

 F - A

Exit at the next road bridge to head back towards Sandbach along Crewe Rd, using road cycle lanes for some of the way - though care is still needed as you are now mixing with busier, faster traffic. At the first main roundabout head across the A533 and bear R back to Sandbach Town Hall and your start point.

Classic English countryside near Church Lawton

Along the Way

Crosses & Canals

For **Sandbach** and **Hassall Green** see Chapter 4.

Leave the ride at Rode Heath, head towards Scholar Green and you will find **Rode Hall**, a magnificent country house and gardens and a large lake set in landscaped parkland. Tearooms. Telephone 01270 873237 or see www.rodehall.co.uk for details. Admission charge.

The stretch of the ride along the **Trent & Mersey Canal** has much of interest including an aqueduct and the unusual Lawton Treble Locks. The **Red Bull** public house at the end of the route with its delightful lockside beer garden makes a relaxing stop before heading back.

The **Salt Line**, a railpath for walkers, cyclists and horse riders on the return leg of the ride, is so named as initially, as part of the Sandbach line of the North Staffordshire Railway Company, it was used mainly for the transport of salt from Northwich and Middlewich to The Potteries. Rich in flora and fauna.

The **Wheelock Rail Trail** from Malkin's Bank is also open to walkers, cyclists and horse riders and forms part of National Cycle Network Route 5.

Well-surfaced canal towpath takes you past distant views of Mow Cop Castle, which you can read about in the previous ride

The famed ancient crosses near your start in Sandbach

West of Winsford

Route Info

Weaver & Whitegate (Easy)
21 miles / 34 km
Off - road   10.5miles / 17km
Height Ascended 358m / 1175ft
Suggested Start Rilshaw Meadows car park, just south of Winsford.
Route Advice NCN route 5, along the Weaver west of Winsford, and the Whitegate Way are good quality dedicated cycle track but elsewhere you use either quiet roads or bridleways with a decent enough surface. The bridleway section west of Newgate Common has a few soft, sandy patches that might mean dismounting and walking.
Nearest Train Station Winsford station is less than 0.25 miles from the route start.
Parking Bottom Flash car park, just south of Winsford.
Food & Drink Red Lion pub en route in Winsford. Egerton Arms and Red Lion pubs in the attractive village of Little Budworth.

Waterside riding near Winsford

Along the Way

Weaver & Whitegate

Winsford Flashes were formed through subsidence caused by the collapse of underground caverns following brine pumping. Bottom Flash, much used for sailing and fishing, lies below **Rilshaw Meadows** at the start of the route, a country park type of area with nice views over the flash. **Winsford**, like some of its neighbours is very much a salt town.

The River Weaver was canalised to allow the transport of salt, and today the **Weaver Cycleway** runs alongside very pretty stretches of river and past impressive salt heaps and works.

Whitegate is pretty too, especially St. Mary's Church. The **Whitegate Way**, another railpath which owes its existence to the transport of salt by rail, has useful facilities at the former Whitegate station - a picnic area, toilets and a 'self-service' information point.

Little Budworth has a shop and post office and two pubs, not to mention a country park and there can be great sunsets over Budworth Pool. If you don't know it's there, the roar of engines from nearby **Oulton Park** motor racing circuit can come as a bit of a surprise.

Visit the area in summer and, as in some other parts of Cheshire, you are likely to see some fantastic and elaborate **scarecrows** erected outside people's houses, at farm entrances etc. as family entries in scarecrow competitions.

Little Budworth, on the southern part of the ride

103

WEAVER & WHITEGATE

A - B Turn L out of Rilshaw Meadows car park onto the road and very shortly turn L onto an off-road path (Weaver Cycleway). Descend steeply to the lakeside, following route 5 signs for Northwich). Pass a sculpture and follow the good quality path to pass under then over two roads to arrive at the Red Lion pub. Route 5 heads down the side and back of the pub, marked Weaver Cycleway. The route parallels the river and, after a ninety degree left-hand bend by the river, splits where you follow a newer, higher path (the riverside path here is dangerous and narrow) looking out for the Union Salt works over to your L. Shortly come to a double bridge over the Weaver.

B - C Head L across both bridges and bear R onto a minor road. Cross a bridge signed 'weak bridge' then climb onto a long, wide straight road into Whitegate. At a T-junction by St Mary's church go L.

WEAVER &
WHITEGATE
Grade - Easy

Note on scale: Each blue-lined grid square is 1 kilometre (about 0.6 miles) across

© Crown copyright and/or database right. All rights reserved. Licence number 100040135

DIRECTIONS NOTE:

R = right

L = left

S/O = straight over

C - D Climb a long hill into tiny Foxwist Green. Go R and immediate L at the crossroads onto Sandy Lane, passing a nice wooden sculpture on the way. At the end of Sandy Lane turn R at the T-junction and follow a road which becomes a track after The Paddocks development. This long sandy road (can be too soft for riding in places in the later stages) arrives at a crossroads where you turn L. Just over the next bridge go L down a ramp to head onto the Whitegate Way, signed Whitegate Station. Leave the track at Whitegate station and R up to the road and L onto it. Descend past Marton House and Coach Rd Farm on the R, turn R just after a sharp R-hand bend. Climb, then pass Shay's Farm on the L. Turn L at the next T-junction onto Longstone Lane. Take the first R and S/O the main A54 (TAKE CARE) onto White Hall Lane, by Little Budworth Methodist Church. Take the first R along Beech Rd. At the next junction go S/O onto a track signed public path (BEWARE SOFT SAND).

D - A At a track crossroads (signed public path in all directions) go L. Keep on this wide track (sandy and puddled in places but perfectly rideable) and meet a road. Go to Little Budworth and follow this road past Oulton Park, ignoring turnings, to come into Little Budworth by the Egerton Arms. After the Red Lion bend L, following the main road as it becomes Mill Lane. In about 1 mile along Mill Lane go R at a crossroads, signed Whitegate & Winsford, onto Park Road. S/O the A54 (TAKE CARE) follow Clay Lane and keep on this road all the way until Whitegate Station. Pick up the Whitegate Way towards Winsford. At the end of the Whitegate Way you meet a road. The longer, more scenic option heads L and back to the double bridge over the Weaver from where you can retrace your tracks alongside the river to your start. Going R at the end of the Whitegate Way, a shorter but less pleasant option, will bring you to a major roundabout where you go L over the river and back to the Red Lion in Winsford, from where you can retrace your outward route.

The double bridge where you cross the Weaver

105

On the towpath near Christleton - Hockenhull Platts ride, following chapte

Tarvin & Tattenhall

Route Info

Hockenhull Platts (Easy)
9.5 miles / 15 km
Off - road 2.5 miles / 4km
Height Ascended 92m / 303ft
Suggested Start Tarvin High Street
Route Advice The off-road sections are generally pretty good and should present few problems for children or beginners in dry weather. There are cobbles over the bridges at Hockenhull Platts but don't let this put you off as they are unmissable. The towpath between Christleton and Waverton is well-surfaced. Roads are generally very quiet. The road from Waverton to Cross Lanes is a little busier and faster.
Nearest Train Station Mouldsworth, about 3 miles away.
Parking Tarvin
Food & Drink Tarvin has a couple of pubs, a delicatessen, cafe and greengrocers. At Christleton the Plough and the Ring O' Bells do pub food as do the Old Trooper and Cheshire Cat pubs by the canal, just through the village.

Mid-Cheshire Villages (Medium)
19 miles / 30.5 km
Off - road 0miles
Height Ascended 381m / 1250ft
Suggested Start Tarvin High Street
Route Advice Virtually all roads but few very busy ones (Tarporley centre is the exception but traffic thins out rapidly once away from the centre). Some fine villages with the hardest climb being to Kelsall, rewarded by lovely views and a visit to the beautifully situated Boot Inn.
Nearest Train Station Mouldsworth, about 3 miles away.
Parking Tarvin
Food & Drink Plenty in Tarporley. Nice pubs at Eaton and Cotebrook. The Summer Trees tea room before coming into Kelsall is in a delightful spot. There are lots of nice pubs in Kelsall, the pick of which is the delightful Boot Inn.

The Boot Inn - en-route in Kelsall - Mid~Cheshire Villages ride

One of Tarporley's lavish shopfronts -
Mid~Cheshire Villages ride

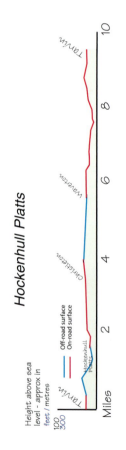

Hockenhull Platts

Height above sea
level - approx in
feet / metres

100
300

Miles

Tarvin

Hockenhull
Platts

Christleton

Waverton

Tarvin

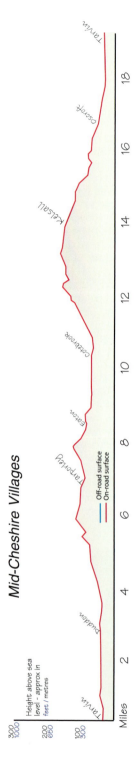

Mid-Cheshire Villages

Height above sea
level - approx in
feet / metres

300
1000

200
650

100
300

Miles

Tarvin

Duddon

Tarporley

Eaton

Cotebrook

Kelsall

Oscroft

Tarvin

Off-road surface
On-road surface

Along the Way

Hockenhull Platts

Tarvin is a nice village at the start of the ride with an excellent cafe and two pubs.
There are great views of the Peckforton Hills and the Welsh hills from **Platts Lane** as it
goes down to **Hockenhull Platts**, an area of meadowland lying around the packhorse
trail which forms the early part of the ride. Some medieval bridges (one pictured on the
back of this book), known as The Roman Bridges, cross the River Gowy here. Nearby
Hockenhull Hall, not accessible to the public, was the home of a servant lady beheaded by
Roundheads whose ghost is said to walk the bridges, amongst other places. See Chapter
5 for **Christleton**.
The **Shropshire Union Canal** was formed by the amalgamation in 1846 of a number of
canals, amongst them this section, part of the then Chester Canal, built in the 1770s.

Mid-Cheshire Villages

Tarvin as above. **Tarporley** is a busy and photogenic little town with a variety of nice
shops and eateries and facilities such as banking, post office and public toilets.
Eaton is pretty with the Red Lion pub just nearby on Beech Lane (01829 732263).
Also just near the ride, at **Cotebrook**, is the Alvanley Arms (01829 760200) and the
Cotebrook Shire Horse Centre where you can see the horses plus a range of wildlife and
farmyard animals and birds (01829 760506).
Kelsall has shops - Co-Op Village Store, a butcher's - and pubs. There's a farm shop at
Eddisbury Fruit Farm, just north of Kelsall on Yeld Lane (01829 759157) and should you
chance to be there on the third Saturday in the month, they have a farmer's market.

One of the medieval bridges at Hockenhull Platts - Hockenhull Platts ride

HOCKENHULL PLATTS

A - B Head down Tarvin High St with the George and Dragon pub behind you on your F then turn L onto Hockenhull Lane and follow it to where it bends R to become Crossfields. Turn L here to continue on Hockenhull Lane, a narrow tarmac lane. Go straight through a bridleway gate then a farm gate to go S/O the BUSY & FAST A51, to continue on the road opposite marked as a dead end. At the right hand bend carry straight on past the egg factory on the L, to pick up the stony track into open countryside with great views. At the track T-junction turn R and continue over the amazing medieval bridges that cross the marshy waters of the River Gowy.

B - C Join a tarmac road and climb past Cotton Farm to a T-junction to go L. Just past the Plough pub go S/O at the crossroads and come into Christleton. Pass Christleton High School then go R at the T-junction into the village centre. Split L just past the Ring O' Bells pub. L at the T-junction by the church. Out of the village pass the College of Law on your R.

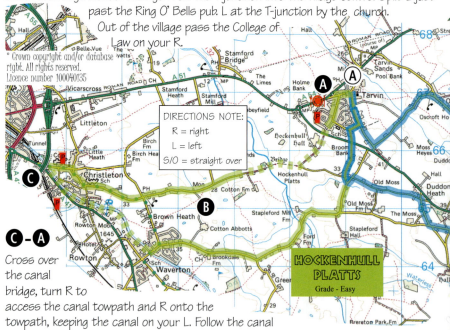

DIRECTIONS NOTE:
R = right
L = left
S/O = straight over

HOCKENHULL PLATTS
Grade - Easy

Crown copyright and/or database right. All rights reserved.
Licence number 100040135

C - A Cross over the canal bridge, turn R to access the canal towpath and R onto the towpath, keeping the canal on your L. Follow the canal towpath until you meet bridge 119. Head R to cross over the canal on this bridge and into Waverton. Follow the road out of Waverton (Guy Lane) for about 2.5 miles then turn L signed for Tarvin and Oscroft. Take the first L onto Broomheath Lane, signed dead end. Ignore the L turn to Sheaf Farm Shop and follow this road to cross S/O the BUSY & FAST A51, into Tarvin. Turn R on at the next T-junction to stay on Broomheath Lane ther L at the next T-junction to head back into Tarvin village centre.

D - A continued.

After descending past the Boot Inn go R at the next junction, signed Tarvin & Oscroft and follow this road for about 1.7 miles to Oscroft. Take the first L in Oscroft. Head out of Oscroft, passing Oscroft Hall. Pass over a small bridge and about 0.85 miles after leaving Oscrofy bear R onto Tarporley Road to bring you back into Tarvin.

MID-CHESHIRE VILLAGES

(A) - (B) From Tarvin High St bend R onto Church St and pass the church on your L. Shortly turn R onto Broomheath Lane then turn first L to keep following Broomheath Lane. TAKE CARE crossing the BUSY & FAST A51 picking up Broomheath Lane again. At the T-junction go L onto Cross Lanes. Take the next R, signed for Duddon and continue to a crossroads at the end of Platts Lane and turn R and L at the next crossroads, signed Duddon. Meet the A51 and CROSS WITH CARE onto Willington Rd. Pass two lots of crossroads and at the third in about 2.25 miles turn R at the end of Wood Lane, signed for Tarporley. Follow this road to cross over the A51 on a bridge and carry on to come to a T-junction where you turn L to visit Tarporley centre.

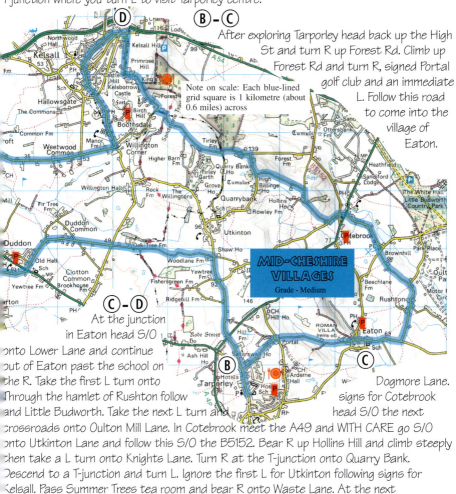

(B) - (C) After exploring Tarporley head back up the High St and turn R up Forest Rd. Climb up Forest Rd and turn R, signed Portal golf club and an immediate L. Follow this road to come into the village of Eaton.

Note on scale: Each blue-lined grid square is 1 kilometre (about 0.6 miles) across

MID-CHESHIRE VILLAGES
Grade - Medium

(C) - (D) At the junction in Eaton head S/O onto Lower Lane and continue out of Eaton past the school on the R. Take the first L turn onto Dogmore Lane. signs for Cotebrook head S/O the next crossroads onto Oulton Mill Lane. In Cotebrook meet the A49 and WITH CARE go S/O onto Utkinton Lane and follow this S/O the B5152. Bear R up Hollins Hill and climb steeply then take a L turn onto Knights Lane. Turn R at the T-junction onto Quarry Bank. Descend to a T-junction and turn L. Ignore the first L for Utkinton following signs for Kelsall. Pass Summer Trees tea room and bear R onto Waste Lane. At the next crossroads turn L by the Farmers Arms pub as you come into Kelsall.

Through the hamlet of Rushton follow and Little Budworth. Take the next L turn and

(D) - (A) Turn R onto Old Coach Road and follow it to a T-junction. Turn L (pubs and village store to R here). Very shortly turn R onto Church St then L onto Willington Lane. Straight over the next crossroads pass Boothsdale on the L which leads to the lovely Boot Inn.

(cont. opposite)

Around Wrenbury

Route Info

Wrenbury Loops (Easy)
North 7 miles / 11 km *South* 8 miles / 13 km
Off - road *North* 0 miles *South* 0 miles
Height Ascended *North* 69m / 225ft *South* 99m /325ft
Suggested Start Wrenbury village centre
Route Advice This corner of Cheshire is full of quiet roads which both these rides use. Although they are relatively short you can combine the two in succession easily enough for a total day's riding of 15 miles.
Nearest Train Station Wrenbury
Parking Wrenbury
Food & Drink Pubs with food and a village store in Wrenbury and a pub-cum-restaurant at Marbury.

An Open Secret (Medium)
15 miles / 24 km
Off - road 0 miles
Height Ascended 127m / 416ft
Suggested Start Wrenbury village centre
Route Advice More quiet roads (just one section of major road to contend with into Audlem).
Nearest Train Station Wrenbury
Parking Wrenbury
Food & Drink Pubs and a village store in Wrenbury. The Bhurtpore Inn at Aston. Lots of choice in Audlem which has a couple of lovely pubs down by the Shropshire Union Canal. There is a cafe at Hack Green Nuclear Bunker (you need to pay the admission fee to use it - worth it as it's a fascinating, if sobering, place).

Wrenbury Loop North

Wrenbury Loop South

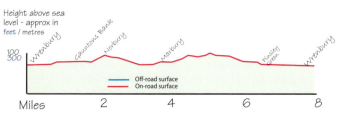

Visit this Cold War relic - An Open Secret ride

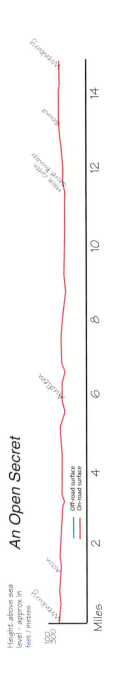

An Open Secret

Height above sea
level - approx in
feet / metres

100
300

Miles

Off-road surface
On-road surface

Wrenbury
Aston
Audlem
Hack Green
Secret Bunker
Sound
Wrenbury

Alongside the Shropshire Union Canal -
An Open Secret ride

WRENBURY LOOPS - NORTHERN LOOP

A - B Head out of Wrenbury centre along the main road (Nantwich Rd), passing the post office and church on your R. Just over the canal turn L onto a lovely road back alongside the canal on your L.. Follow this road, following signs for Norbury and Bickley to Gauntons Bank and there turn L onto the road of the same name, signed Norbury & Marbury.

B - A In Norbury come to a T-junction and turn R. Turn R at the next T-junction and continue to Swanwick Green. Carry S/O here, signed Bickley & Whitchurch, ignoring the R for Norbury and Wrenbury. Turn first R just out of Swanwick Green onto Snab Lane and next R onto Common Lane which will bring you into Norbury Common. At the next crossroads turn L onto Holtridge Lane (signed for NCN cycle route 45). At the staggered crossroads at the end of Holtridge Lane turn R, signed for Wrenbury & Sound. Simply follow this road for around 2 miles, ignoring a L turn along the way, to come over the canal and back into the centre of Wrenbury.

Crown copyright and/or database right. All rights reserved. Licence number 100040135

WRENBURY LOOPS - SOUTHERN LOOP

A - B As in the Northern Loop described above.

B - C In Norbury come to a T-junction and turn L onto School Lane, signed Marbury. Follow this very quiet road into Marbury. At the T-junction here turn L, signed Whitchurch, onto Wirswall Rd. In the centre of this tiny village bear R onto Hollins Lane by the Swan Inn.

C - A Take the first minor L about 0.75 miles out of Marbury, signed Hollyhurst & Marley Green. Follow this road (Hollyhurst Rd) to pass under the railway, ignoring the R turn signed for Whitchurch. Stay on Hollyhurst Rd all the way to its end, near Yew Tree Farm, just after it passes back under the railway. Go R at this T-junction following signs for Pinsley Green & Wrenbury. Stay on this road for just over a mile, ignoring the R to Aston, to come back into Wrenbury. Head R at the T-junction back to the centre.

DIRECTIONS NOTE:
R = right
L = left
S/O = straight over

N OPEN SECRET

(A) - (B) From Wrenbury centre head away from the post office on your L and take a R
urn onto Station Road, signed Wrenbury Station, Aston & Audlem. Follow this road past
he train station on the L and bend L, ignoring a minor R turn (Pinsley Green Rd). Bear R
to Aston and pass the Bhurtpore Inn, following the road to the A530. Head S/O here,
ollowing signs for Wilkesley & Audlem. After 1.2 miles turn L onto Back Coole Lane, signed
rown's Bank & Audlem. Follow this road to its end at the T-junction with Coole Lane.
o visit Audlem turn R here then turn L on meeting the A525 (TAKE CARE). This will bring
ou to Audlem's delightful centre. To rejoin the main route retrace your tracks to the
nction of Coole Lane and Back Coole Lane and continue north on Coole Lane, passing
Back Coole Lane on
the L.

Note on scale: Each blue-lined
grid square is 1 kilometre (about
0.6 miles) across

(B) - (A)
ollow Coole
ane to cross over
he Shropshire Union
anal by Coole Hall Farm
&B sign. 1.4 miles after
rossing the canal turn L, signed
ecret Bunker, onto French Lane. Hack Green
ecret Bunker is shortly on your L (see Along
he Way). After a visit here continue on over
he canal and follow Mickley Hall Lane to its end and turn R
t this unsigned junction. Follow cycle route 75 signs, to the main A530. Here follow signs
r Nantwich, route 75 and immediate R onto New Town Rd. Go R at the next junction,
ow in Sound, signed route 75. Bear L on the edge of Sound to pick up Wrenbury Heath
d, signed Wrenbury Heath and Wrenbury. Cross over the railway and at the next
taggered crossroads head S/O. This will bring you to a T-junction opposite Wrenbury Hall
here you go L back to Wrenbury.

AN OPEN
SECRET
Grade - Medium

Along the Way

Wrenbury Loops

Wrenbury is an excellent start/finish point for these rides. Its railway station is on the line from Crewe and Nantwich in one direction and Whitchurch and Shrewsbury in the other. There's a shop and post office, a brewery with a bar and two nice canalside pubs - the Cotton Arms (has a campsite - see chapter 4) and the Dusty Miller by the unusual lifting road bridge (also see Chapter 4). See the village's website www.wrenbury.info for lots of local information (and photos of some of the scarecrows people build in the summer competition - they really are amazing).

Swanwick Green on the Northern Loop is a very pretty little hamlet.

On the Southern Loop, the Llangollen Branch of the Shropshire Union Canal comes down from Wrenbury to cross the ride north of picturesque **Marbury** and is worth a stop. The renowned Swan Inn at Marbury (01948 662220) is on the route.

South of the ride between Marbury and Wrenbury is the **Comber Mere Monument**, a tall stone structure in memory of Field Marshall Viscount Combermere who died in the 19th century (Combermere Abbey lies about a mile beyond that - access through group tours, special events or cottage hire only).

An Open Secret

The Bhurtpore Inn (01270 780917) was built by Baron Combermere following his taking in India in 1826 of the fortress city of Bhurtpore following the local rajah's conflict with the East India Company.

At Aston, a range of pottery is in the shop at **The Firs Pottery** (01270 780345).

See Chapter 4 for **Audlem** and **Hack Green Nuclear Bunker**, both well worth taking time out for.

Wrenbury Hall, now used for weddings and functions, was used by Parliamentarian forces in the Civil War prior to the Battle of Nantwich.

Quiet lanes round Wrenbury are great for families - Wrenbury Loops ride

Around Malpas

Route Info

On The Bishop's Trail 1 (Easy)
7.5 miles / 12 km
Off - road 1.2 miles / 2 km
Height Ascended 134m / 440ft
Suggested Start Malpas centre
Route Advice A short but sweet circuit around the lovely town of Malpas. The off-road sections are of the green lane variety - generally grassy but wide, with an even foundation for riding. As with most bridleway riding though the condition can vary according to the weather, time of year and the amount of recent use the track has had.
Nearest Train Stations Whitchurch station is about 5.5 miles away, Wrenbury a little more.
Parking Malpas
Food & Drink Plenty of opportunities in Malpas, including the excellent Creation Station cafe in the old fire station.

Dymock's Mill (Medium)
9.5 miles / 15km
Off - road About 0.5 miles
Height Ascended 165m / 542ft
Suggested Start Malpas centre
Route Advice More undulating countryside to the south-west of Malpas along lightly-trafficked roads and dipping over the Welsh border. A steep climb into and out of Wych Brook is the only major challenge of the ride - it's technically 'off-road' but the surface is excellent.
Nearest Train Stations Whitchurch station is about 5.5 miles away, Wrenbury a little more.
Parking Malpas
Food & Drink Threapwood Post Office has various snack foods and is open daily. The pub at Sarn Bridge also does food.

Cholmondeley Castle (Medium)
11 miles / 17.5km
Off - road About 1.2 miles / 2 km
Height Ascended 201m / 660ft
Suggested Start Malpas centre
Route Advice There are some faster roads mixed with the quiet back roads on this slightly longer ride. Coming back into Malpas you use the off-road sections of the ride *On The Bishop's Trail 1,* so note the comments there about the off-road sections. If you are visiting Cholmondeley Castle you can use the suggested extension shown on the map which will let you exit via the estate road.
Nearest Train Stations Whitchurch station is about 5.5 miles away, Wrenbury a little more.
Parking Malpas
Food & Drink No Man's Heath has the Wheatsheaf pub. Cholmondeley Castle Farm shop serves hot pies, cakes and a variety of snack food (hot food 10-2)

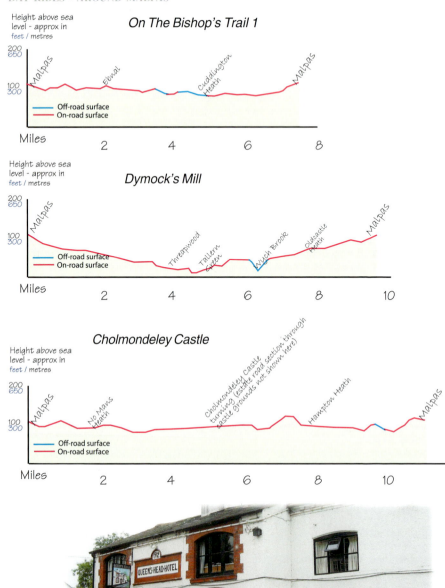

Height above sea
level - approx in
feet / *metres*

On The Bishop's Trail 1

200
650

100
300

Malpas

Ebnal

Cuddington
Heath

Malpas

— Off-road surface
— On-road surface

Miles   2   4   6   8

Height above sea
level - approx in
feet / metres

Dymock's Mill

200
650

100
300

Malpas

Threapwood

Tallern
Green

Wych Brook

Oldcastle
Heath

Malpas

— Off-road surface
— On-road surface

Miles   2   4   6   8   10

Cholmondeley Castle

Height above sea
level - approx in
feet / metres

200
650

100
300

Malpas

No Mans
Heath

Cholmondeley Castle
turning (estate road section through
castle grounds not shown here)

Hampton Heath

Malpas

— Off-road surface
— On-road surface

Miles   2   4   6   8   10

A great place for a break on the Dymock's Mill ride

Bishop's Trail byways; south and north of Overton Heath (top and bottom respectively)

ON THE BISHOP'S TRAIL 1

(A)-(B) With Church St and the Cross over to your R head down the main street in Malpas and turn L onto Springfield Rd. Turn R at the next T-junction and leave Malpas. After about 1 mile turn L onto Ebnal Lane. Continue to Ebnal and bear R to the B5069 where you head R then immediate L onto Mates Lane. At the next junction turn L and as the road bends L take the track on your R signed Byway, following the line of the road you have left (there is also a byway signed for Tilston on your R at this junction which you ignore). Follow this wide track until it emerges at Overton Heath Lane where you turn R. In about 0.4 miles turn R onto a well-made track marked as the Bishop Bennet Way signed for Cuddington Heath.

Follow this byway to emerge at a road and turn R.

(B)-(A) Shortly turn L in Cuddington Heath to the B5069 and R again. Go first L, signed Oldcastle, onto a minor road. Head S/O at the next crossroads In Oldcastle Heath go L at the T-junction. Follow this road to the B5395 and turn L back into Malpas.

ON THE BISHOP'S TRAIL 1
Grade - Easy

DIRECTIONS NOTE
R = right
L = left
S/O = straight over

DYMOCK'S MILL

A-B In Malpas find the Cross by the Crown Hotel and turn up Church Street.

Follow this road (the B5069) past the church to the edge of Malpas and turn L by

DYMOCK'S MILL
Grade - Medium

the phone box onto a minor road (Sunnyside). Head S/O the next crossroads and shortly after this go R at another crossroads. Follow this road for 2 miles into Upper Threapwood

B-A Turn L at the T-junction with Chapel Lane here and L at the next T-junction, signed Sarn. Follow this road which leads to Sarn Bridge and the delightful Queens Head pub, with its waterwheel and lovely beer garden. Climb over Wych Brook and bear L, signed Tallern Green and Whitchurch, to come into Wales. Carry on out of the village, ignoring the R turn and following signs for Tybroughton and Lower Wych. 0.6 miles out of Tallern Green turn L down an unsigned gravel track which descends past The Woodlands to a lovely private residence at Dymock's Mill complete with mill pond. Over Wych Brook climb very steeply, onto tarmac to a T-junction and R. Through Oldcastle Heath continue to Malpas.

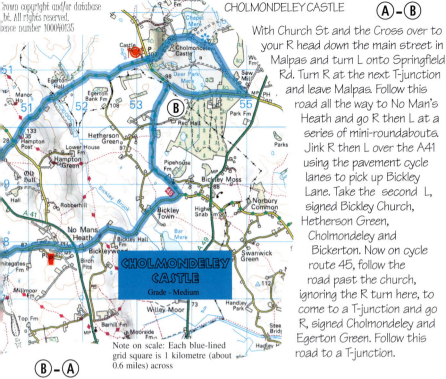

Crown copyright and/or database right. All rights reserved. Licence number 100040135

CHOLMONDELEY CASTLE   Ⓐ - Ⓑ

With Church St and the Cross over to your R head down the main street in Malpas and turn L onto Springfield Rd. Turn R at the next T-junction and leave Malpas. Follow this road all the way to No Man's Heath and go R then L at a series of mini-roundabouts. Jink R then L over the A41 using the pavement cycle lanes to pick up Bickley Lane. Take the second L, signed Bickley Church, Hetherson Green, Cholmondeley and Bickerton. Now on cycle route 45, follow the road past the church, ignoring the R turn here, to come to a T-junction and go R, signed Cholmondeley and Egerton Green. Follow this road to a T-junction.

CHOLMONDELEY CASTLE

Grade - Medium

Note on scale: Each blue-lined grid square is 1 kilometre (about 0.6 miles) across

Ⓑ - Ⓐ

To visit Cholmondeley Castle go R at this junction (if not you can short-cut by going L, signed Egerton Green & Bickerton). After just under a mile turn L into the main entrance to Cholmondeley Castle. Follow the lovely access drive past the pay point - you must pay to enter if you want to take this route option. After a look round this beautiful site, follow the exit road to emerge at the road just down from the estate's farm shop (see Food & Drink pg 117). Head S/O here and simply follow the road for around 2.4 miles, passing a couple of fisheries on the way. It becomes Cholmondeley Rd and hits the A41. Go S/O here WITH CARE then L onto the B5069 which will re-enter Malpas as Chester Rd. Meet the High St and go L back to Malpas centre.

Barely a straight line on this building in Malpas

Along the Way

Historic **Malpas** is a good start/finish for these rides with places to eat and shop and accommodation if you need it. A good number of half-timbered buildings give the place a real 'old England' feel. See Chapter 4 for more details.

On the Bishop's Trail 1
Bishop Bennet Way is named after William Bennet, a late 18th / early 19th century bishop who surveyed some of the old Roman roads of England, including those between Chester and Whitchurch.

Dymock's Mill
If you're feeling adventurous, you can try and find the old tower windmill at **Threapwood**, a quite large but spread-out village, and then reward your efforts with a break at the **Queen's Head** at Sarn (01948 770244), right on the Welsh border. Nice beer garden. **Dymock's Mill** is a private house with mill pond in a lovely valley-bottom setting. **The Wheatsheaf** at No Mans Heath is a pleasant country pub (01948 820337).

Cholmondeley Castle
Cholmondeley Castle is not open to the public, but its wonderful gardens are, along with a tearoom and a programme of special events. Admission charge. Telephone 01829 720383. Just near the ride, the **Cholmondeley Castle Farm Shop** has refreshments - see Chapter 4 for details.

The Creation Station cafe, Malpas - once a different kind of station

Tattenhall & The Peckfortons

Route Info

On the Bishop's Trail 2 (Easy)
12 miles / 19km
Off - road 2.75 miles / 4.5km
Height Ascended 131m / 430ft
Suggested Start Farndon High Street
Route Advice This ride has one of the finest green lanes in Cheshire on your approach to Churton.
Nearest Train Station Chester train station is just over 7 miles from Churton down the B5130.
Parking Plenty of parking in Farndon.
Food & Drink There are three pubs in Farndon and the lovely Vernon's coffee shop nearby in Holt. Soft drinks, crisps etc. at Stretton Watermill.

Peckfortons North (Medium)
16 miles / 26km
Off - road About 0.4 miles / 0.6km
Height Ascended 276m / 906ft
Suggested Start Tattenhall High Street
Route Advice Watch out for the very bumpy cobbled section after Higher Burwardsley.
Nearest Train Station Chester train station is about 7.5 miles from Tattenhall.
Parking Tattenhall.
Food & Drink Tattenhall offers several pubs, several food shops and even an Indian restaurant. The classy Pheasant Inn at Higher Burwardsley is a fantastic location for a meal whilst the village hall at Peckforton offers tea and an information point. There are some lovely pubs at or near Bunbury, including the Yew Tree, Nags Head and Dysart Arms plus a village store and even a chippy!

Peckfortons South (Medium)
12 miles / 19km
Off - road 0 miles
Height Ascended 285m /935 ft
Suggested Start Tattenhall High Street
Route Advice All on road - mainly minor ones.
Nearest Train Station Chester train station is about 7.5 miles from Tattenhall.
Parking Tattenhall.
Food & Drink Tattenhall offers several pubs, several food shops and even an Indian restaurant. There are fewer refreshment stops along the way as the southern Peckfortons are less on the tourist trail - in fact there is just one pub, The Coppermine, at Fullers Moor and it does food daily (see Chapter 5 for details).

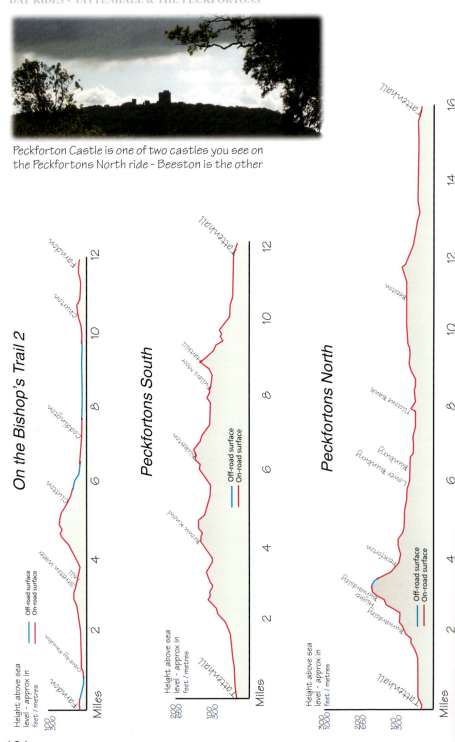

Peckforton Castle is one of two castles you see on the Peckfortons North ride - Beeston is the other

On the Bishop's Trail 2

Height above sea
level - approx in
feet / metres
100
300

Off-road surface
On-road surface

Farndon · Crewe by Farndon · Stretton Water Mill · Clutton · Coddington · Clutton · Churton · Farndon

Miles · 2 · 4 · 6 · 8 · 10 · 12

Peckfortons South

Height above sea
level - approx in
feet / metres
200 650
100 300

Off-road surface
On-road surface

Tattenhall · Brown Knowl · Bickerton · Fuller's Moor · Harthill · Tattenhall

Miles · 2 · 4 · 6 · 8 · 10 · 12

Peckfortons North

Height above sea
level - approx in
feet / metres
300 1000
200 650
100 300

Off-road surface
On-road surface

Tattenhall · Burwardsley · Higher Burwardsley · Peckforton · Lower Bunbury · Bunbury · Tilstone Bank · Beeston · Tattenhall

Miles · 2 · 4 · 6 · 8 · 10 · 12 · 14 · 16

Along the Way

On the Bishop's Trail 2
Between them, **Holt**, in Wales, and **Farndon** have a good number of nice and useful shops and places to eat and drink. There's a picnic area down by the river by the bridge over the Dee, on the border with Wales. Like many places in the area, the village has Civil War connections - the bridge was fought over by the Roundheads and the Royalists. The cartographer John Speed (1542 - 1629) was born here. Coming back into Farndon at the end of the ride, you pass the impressive **Barnston Monument**, erected to Roger Barnston, a nineteenth century soldier who served in the Crimea and in India.
See Chapter 5 for details of **Stretton Watermill**.
At **Lower Carden**, you will see one of the impressive lodges to Carden Hall, an ancient half timbered house which burned down in 1912 and is now the site of a hotel and golf courses. A shelter on the estate is thought to have been home to John Harris, an 18th century cave-dweller who took to a hermit's life as a result of unrequited love.
Coddington has the lovely parish church of St. Mary the Virgin. Also to be found there is Manor Wood Country Caravan Park - see Chapter 5 for details.
The **Bishop Bennet Way**, a long distance horse riding route, is delightful.
Churton has the White Horse pub (01829 270208).

Peckfortons North
Tattenhall and **Burwardsley** - see Chapter 5. There are fine views as you cross over the Peckforton Hills, not least from the garden of the Pheasant Inn at Higher Burwardsley. The Malpas Loop of **The National Byway** runs through the hills and is waymarked with the occasional plaque giving interesting local information - The National Byway is a four thousand mile leisure cycle route linking heritage sites - see www.thenationalbyway.org. Crossing this ride as it runs along the Peckforton Hills is **The Sandstone Trail**, a walkers' route running from Whitchurch to Frodsham. When you pass the **Yew Tree Inn** (01829 260274), you come into **Bunbury**, another of those lovely, lively little villages with nice shops and pubs and thatched black and white cottages where you might not feel surprised to see Miss Marple coming out of the post office. The church of St. Boniface is striking.
Bunbury Water Mill is a restored nineteenth century cornmill, open Sundays and Bank Holiday Mondays part of the year - see www.bunbury-mill.org.
The ruins of **Beeston Castle** dominate the landscape for miles around - see Chapter 5 for details.

Peckfortons South
Tattenhall, Harthill and **Burwardsley** - see Chapter 5.
Not normally open to the public, **Bolesworth Castle** was built in 1828 and modernised to plans by Clough Williams Ellis, creator of Portmeirion, early in the twentieth century.
The site of **Broxton Old Hall** dates to before Edward III. Alpine cheese is made at Larkton Hall Farm.
Near the ride on the north side of **Bickerton Hill**, a large area of heathland managed by the National Trust along with **Maiden Castle** and **Larkton Hill**, there is **Mad Allen's Hole**, a cave where the hermit John Harris referred to in the Bishop's Trail 2 notes for Carden Hall may have had a second home, the cave maybe being named after a later occupant.

In mid-summer the byway between Clutton & Coddington is a delight - On the Bishop's Trail 2

A-B From Farndon High Street head down Church Street (just about opposite the Post Office). At St Chad's church bear L onto Church Lane and past the car park. Turn R onto Barton Rd and take the next R turn onto Crewe Lane. At the end of the tarmac head S/O through bollards and bridleway gate and cross the busy A534 WITH EXTREME CARE, to pick up the road on the other side which will take you into Crewe-by-Farndon.

B-C In Crewe-by-Farndon head S/O onto Wetreins Lane. In about 1.7 miles, at the T-junction with Stretton Hall up to your L, turn L. Take the next R, past Stretton Old Hall, signed Stretton Water Mill and Carden. Pass Stretton Watermill (see Along the Way) and continue to the T-junction by the impressive red stone gates and turn L, signed Carden.

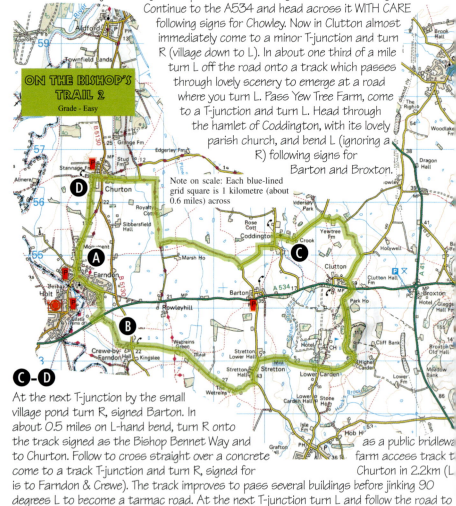

Continue to the A534 and head across it WITH CARE following signs for Chowley. Now in Clutton almost immediately come to a minor T-junction and turn R (village down to L). In about one third of a mile turn L off the road onto a track which passes through lovely scenery to emerge at a road where you turn L. Pass Yew Tree Farm, come to a T-junction and turn L. Head through the hamlet of Coddington, with its lovely parish church, and bend L (ignoring a R) following signs for Barton and Broxton.

ON THE BISHOP'S
TRAIL 2
Grade - Easy

Note on scale: Each blue-lined grid square is 1 kilometre (about 0.6 miles) across

C-D
At the next T-junction by the small village pond turn R, signed Barton. In about 0.5 miles on L-hand bend, turn R onto the track signed as the Bishop Bennet Way and to Churton. Follow to cross straight over a concrete come to a track T-junction and turn R, signed for is to Farndon & Crewe). The track improves to pass several buildings before jinking 90 degrees L to become a tarmac road. At the next T-junction turn L and follow the road to climb into Churton on Pump Lane.

...as a public bridlewa... farm access track t... Churton in 2.2km (L...

D-A At the B5130 head across onto Hob Lane by the White Horse pub. Turn L onto Stannage Lane, leading to the Knowl. Turn R onto a faster road (TAKE CARE) and follow this road past Barnston's Monument back into Farndon.

ECKFORTONS SOUTH

(A)-(B)

ollow the same route as Peckfortons North out of Tattenhall and onto Burwardsley Road.
ust past Birds Lane on the L take the next R, signed Harthill, Broxton and Bolesworth.
ollow Dark Lane to its end and turn L and first R. Climb steeply before levelling out and
escending to the A534. WITH CARE head S/O onto Hill Lane, signed Brown Knowl. At the
junction with Sherrington Lane turn R and continue to the T-junction, opposite Broxton
ld Hall, where you turn L, signed Duckington.

(B)-(C)
Follow this road to come to a crossroads and go L, signed Bickerton. Climb and
descend through tiny Bickerton and go L at the next
crossroads onto Long Lane, signed Broxton. Very shortly turn
L onto the lovely Reading Room Lane. Back in Brown Knowl go
R at the first T-junction you come to. Follow this
road into Fullers Moor and go R at the split, off
Smithy Lane, onto a very minor road to come to the
A534 by the Coppermine pub.

(C)-(A)
Head S/O the A534 WTH CARE signed
Harthill & Burwardsley. Harthill Lane gives great views
of the southern end of the sandstone outcrops of
Raw Head. Follow the road into Harthill and
through this tiny, pretty village
descend then take the first R turn
(NCN routes 70 and 45) signed
Burwardsley. In Burwardsley
follow cycle route signs 45
through the village, onto
Burwardsley Rd, which you
follow all the way back to
Tattenhall.

Link to Peckforton Hills North - see overleaf

PECKFORTON HILLS SOUTH
Grade - Medium

DIRECTIONS NOTE:
R = right
L = left
S/O = straight over

* Crown copyright and/or database
right. All rights reserved.
Licence number 100040135

Stretton Watermill; drop by
as you ride the Bishop's
Trail ride

PECKFORTON HILLS NORTH
Grade - Medium

Link to Peckforton Hills South - see previous page

Note on scale: Each blue-lined grid square is 1 kilometre (about 0.6 miles) across

Crown copyright and/or database right. All rights reserved. Licence number 100040135

PECKFORTONS NORTH

A-B From Tattenhall High St head uphill and past the Sportsmans Arms turn R onto Burwardsley Road (also signed National Cycle Network route 45). Follow this road, ignoring any turnings, to come into Burwardsley. Past the Post Office take the next L onto Church Rd. Pass Sarra Lane on the R and then pass the church. At the end of School Lane turn R and climb steeply. Come into Higher Burwardsley and bend R by the Candle Workshop, onto Fowlers Bench Lane (the Pheasant Inn is down to the L and Barracks Lane is on your R). Very shortly turn L down Rock Lane, marked as a dead end (note the National Byway plaque). At the first split bear R, climbing steeply uphill and at the next junction head S/O, signed Bulkeley Hill (L is to Beeston Castle). Pass the Sandstone Trail to the R and pick up a lovely broad sandstone track.

B-C Cobbles start to show through the sandstone and as you descend under a lovely little bridge the cobbles take over (DISMOUNT ADVISABLE). There are superlative views to your R. Continue descending to pick up the tarmac road and emerge in Peckforton. At the T-junction go R then take the first L onto Peckforton Hall Lane, signed Bunbury. Follow this road all the way to the A49 at Spurstow and jink L then R across it WITH CARE, onto Long Lane, signed Bunbury and Haughton. At the Yew Tree pub turn L, signed Bunbury. Coming into Bunbury ignore the L turn by the village sign (depicting cow and church) and carry on, signed Tarporley. This will bring you into lovely Higher Bunbury.

C-D Bear L then R to pass St Boniface's church on the R, following signs for Bunbury Mill, and continue on this road to pass Bunbury Water Mill (worth a visit - see Along the Way). Continue to Bunbury Commons and turn L. Go R at the next crossroads to visit Tilstone Bank's pretty canal area, then head back to this crossroads and go S/O, signed Bunbury. Back in Higher Bunbury, at the T-junction opposite the church, go R. Retrace your steps to the village sign in Bunbury and turn R, following signs for Beeston. Bear R past the chippy and continue to the A49. Jink L then R CROSSING WITH GREAT CARE, following signs for Beeston, Beeston Castle and Candle Workshops. Follow this road for about a mile to come to a T-junction and go L. Now in Beeston, very shortly turn R, signed Burwardsley, Tattenhall & Beeston Castle. Turn next R, signed Beeston Castle.

D-A Pass Bates Mill Lane on the R, passing under the steep cliff face on which the castle sits, and bend R, following signs for Burwardsley and Tattenhall. Just follow this road for about 2.7 miles (Tattenhall Lane becoming Birds Lane) to a T-junction where you turn R to retrace your steps into Tattenhall.

South of Macclesfield

Route Info

A Jester's Trail (Easy)
13 miles / 21 km
Off - road 0 miles
Height Ascended 187m / 615ft
Suggested Start Gawsworth Hall
Route Advice Despite its proximity to Macclesfield there are still some scenic and relatively quiet roads on which to explore the rolling green countryside of the area. One brief section of main road requires especial care.
Nearest Train Station Macclesfield station is about 3.5 miles from Gawsworth.
Parking Warren village
Food & Drink Harrington Arms at Gawsworth does lunchtime sandwiches and soup. The Davenport Arms at Marton does food and there's also a farm shop and cafe nearby. The Little Acorn Coffee Shop in Holland's Nurseries is a quarter of a mile north on the A536 of where the ride crosses it at Rodeheath.

Along the Way

A Jester's Trail
See Chapter 3 for details of **Gawsworth Hall**.
At **Marton**, the black and white timber framed church, reportedly Europe's oldest timber framed church still in use, dates back to the fourteenth century and has important wall paintings. Nearby is an ancient oak tree, thought to be at least 600 years old.
From the long straight leading to the A523, you get excellent views to the south of **The Cloud**, a large hill (1125 feet) on the border with Staffordshire.
The ride crosses the **Macclesfield Canal** at a couple of points. It was opened in 1831 and was one of the last narrow canals to be built. Bosley Locks, just south of the ride, are twelve locks in one and a quarter miles.

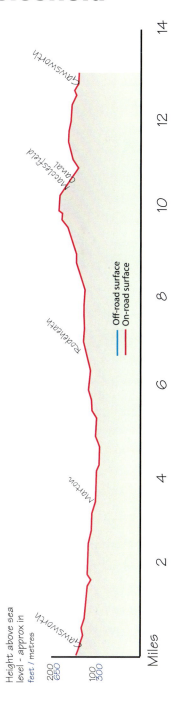

Off-road surface
On-road surface

Height above sea level - approx in feet / metres
200
650
100
300

Miles

A JESTER'S TRAIL

Ⓐ-Ⓑ Head away from Gawsworth Hall as if going towards Warren. At the first crossroads turn L down Maggoty Lane. S/O the A536 follow Marton Lane all the way to Marton. Head across the BUSY AND FAST A34 (the Davenport Arms, farm shop cafe and church are all down to the L here, along the main road) onto Bunce Lane and continue to a T-junction to turn L onto Marton Hall Lane, which takes you past Marton Hall on your L. At the T-junction with the A34 turn L (TAKE CARE - BUSY AND FAST). Shortly, take the next R, signed North Rode, onto Cocksmoss Lane. Follow this road, passing Moss Bank Farm to the A536.

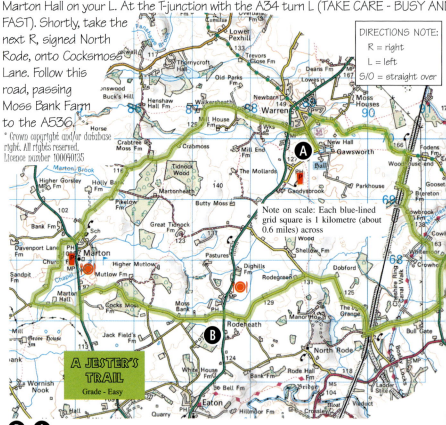

DIRECTIONS NOTE:
R = right
L = left
S/O = straight over

Note on scale: Each blue-lined grid square is 1 kilometre (about 0.6 miles) across

° Crown copyright and/or database right. All rights reserved. Licence number 100040135

A JESTER'S TRAIL
Grade - Easy

Ⓑ-Ⓐ Take care going S/O the A536, signed North Rode & Bosley (BUSY & FAST - but note if you head north on the A536 here for about 0.25 miles you will come to Hollands Nurseries with the Little Acorns Coffee Shop). Back on Pexall Rd bear L at the first junction, signed for Bosley. R at the next junction, signed North Rode and Bosley. Follow this road past Dobford Farm and cross over the railway. Ignore the next R turn, and follow the long straight over the Macclesfield Canal up to the A523. Turn L WITH CARE up this busy and fast road and after 0.5 miles take the first L up Cowbrook Lane. Pass over the Macclesfield Canal again and continue descending past Cowbrook Farm. Climb and pass back over the railway line. Turn L at the next T-junction signed Congleton (A536) & Gawsworth. Now on cycle route 55, drop down towards Warren and take the first L just coming into the village, still NCN 55, and next L to return to Gawsworth Hall.

Gawsworth - home of the poignant jester, Maggoty John, buried nearby

West & North of Chester

Route Info

Animals & Boats (Easy)
20 miles / 32km   Off - road 16 miles / 26km
Height Ascended 140m / 460ft   **Suggested Start** Chester centre
Route Advice Easy and well-surfaced canal towpath plus some minor roads and a nice bridleway section through Chester Zoo.
Nearest Train Station Chester   **Parking** Chester
Food & Drink Lots of options in Chester centre.
The Bunbury Arms at Stoak does food lunchtimes and evenings and all day on Sundays. Cafe at Ellesmere Port Boat Museum (if you're paying to go into the museum).

Deeside Dawdle (Easy)
14 miles / 22.5km
Off - road 14 miles / 22.5km
Height Ascended 50m / 165ft   **Suggested Start** Chester centre
Route Advice A superb family or beginners' route as it is entirely off-road and on wide, good quality dedicated cycle track.
Nearest Train Stations Chester station is near the start and Hawarden Bridge at the halfway point (on the line that serves east Wales and the Wirral).
Parking Chester
Food & Drink Lots of options in Chester centre but nothing on the rest of the route itself, although there are pubs in Queensferry and Blacon.

Once Beside the Seaside (Medium)
32 miles / 51.5km
(A circuit out to Capenhurst and back is 16 miles / 26km)
Off - road 16 miles / 26km
Height Ascended 254.5m / 835ft   **Suggested Start** Chester centre
Route Advice A lengthy but fairly gentle ride on a fifty-fifty mix of mainly quiet roads and good quality off-road trail. Some short but steepish climbs between Burton and Neston
Nearest Train Stations Chester, Bache, Capenhurst and Neston.
Parking Chester
Food & Drink Mollington Meats farm shop sells quality ice cream and other snack food as well as fresh farm products. There is a cafe at Ness Gardens and plenty of places in Neston and Parkgate. The Nag's Head pub is at Willaston (See Chapter 1). The Eureka Cyclists' Cafe at Two Mills is near the route as it heads out of Capenhurst on the return. See details in Chapter 1. Also the Yacht Inn at Woodbank.

Once Beside the Seaside

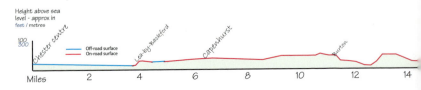

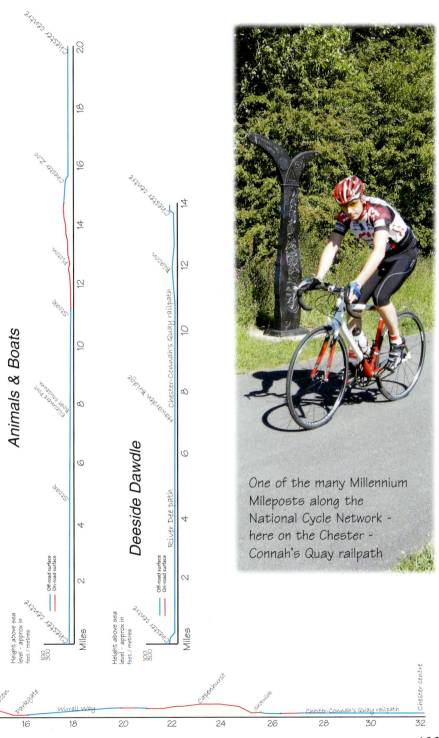

Animals & Boats

Height above sea level - approx in feet / metres

100
300

- Off-road surface
- On-road surface

CHESTER CENTRE · CHESTER CENTRE · STOAK · ELLESMERE PORT BOAT MUSEUM · STOAK · PICTON · CHESTER ZOO · CHESTER CENTRE

Miles: 2 4 6 8 10 12 14 16 18 20

Deeside Dawdle

Height above sea level - approx in feet / metres

100
300

- Off-road surface
- On-road surface

CHESTER CENTRE · River Dee path · Chester-Connah's Quay railpath · Hawarden Bridge · Blacon · CHESTER CENTRE

Miles: 2 4 6 8 10 12 14

One of the many Millennium Mileposts along the National Cycle Network - here on the Chester - Connah's Quay railpath

Neston · Parkgate · Wirral Way · Capenhurst · Shotwick · Chester-Connah's Quay railpath · Chester centre

16 18 20 22 24 26 28 30 32

133

One of several interesting bridges on the Deeside Dawdle route - this one at Higher Ferry

Along the Way

Deeside Dawdle

Powerful sunsets, huge, racing, cloudy skies ; all sorts of dramatic views may be seen from the banking alongside the canalised section of the **River Dee**, especially from the footbridge over the river near Higher Ferry House.

Hawarden railway bridge, dating from1889, is a swing bridge although apparently never opened now. The ride returns along the path of the old railway line from Mickle Trafford to Dee Marsh junction. Once there were stations at Chester, Blacon, Saughall and Sealand and even a halt for the golf club on Sealand marshes, now long defunct - prime minister Gladstone was once President and Captain there.

Once Beside the Seaside

See Chapter 1 for information on places along the earlier part of the ride - Ness Botanic Gardens, Neston, Parkgate, Willaston and food and drink establishments.

Parts of **The Wirral Way** are used as you pass through Parkgate and Neston and the **Wirral Country Park**, which was opened in 1973 along the old railway line from Hooton, once serving Neston, Parkgate and the Wirral.

Like **Burton** to its north-east, **Shotwick** was once a port, the river reaching the church wall. Now, silting means that it's an inland village, and one of the prettiest you're likely to see. The church of St. Michael has a Norman arch and Shotwick Hall (private) was built in 1662.

Animals & Boats

This is a ride with outstanding family attractions. **Ellesmere Port Boat Museum** is in a spectacular location where the Shropshire Union Canal meets the Manchester Ship Canal and the Mersey Estuary. Admission fee
0151 3555017   www.boatmuseum.org.uk

Chester Zoo One of the country's best known zoos with more than 7,000 animals. The route passes right through the middle on a public bridleway and past the entrance. Admission fee   01244 380280   www.chesterzoo.org

Marsh access track at Shotwick

ONCE BESIDE THE SEASIDE

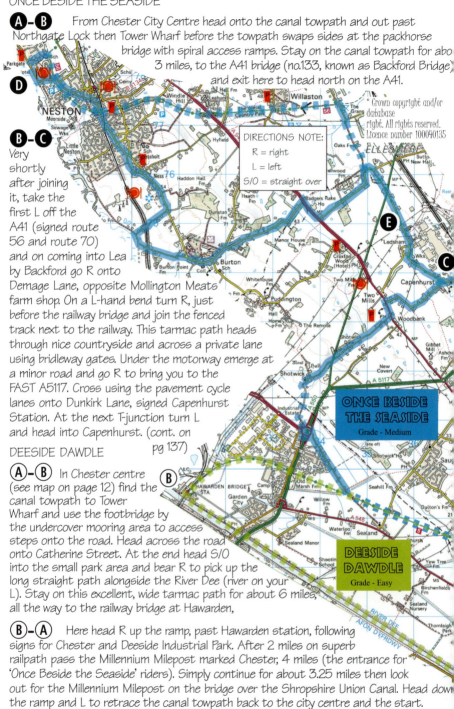

A - B From Chester City Centre head onto the canal towpath and out past Northgate Lock then Tower Wharf before the towpath swaps sides at the packhorse bridge with spiral access ramps. Stay on the canal towpath for abo 3 miles, to the A41 bridge (no.133, known as Backford Bridge) and exit here to head north on the A41.

B - C Very shortly after joining it, take the first L off the A41 (signed route 56 and route 70) and on coming into Lea by Backford go R onto Demage Lane, opposite Mollington Meats farm shop. On a L-hand bend turn R, just before the railway bridge and join the fenced track next to the railway. This tarmac path heads through nice countryside and across a private lane using bridleway gates. Under the motorway emerge at a minor road and go R to bring you to the FAST A5117. Cross using the pavement cycle lanes onto Dunkirk Lane, signed Capenhurst Station. At the next T-junction turn L and head into Capenhurst. (cont. on pg 137)

DIRECTIONS NOTE:
R = right
L = left
S/O = straight over

Crown copyright and/or database right. All rights reserved. Licence number 100040135

ONCE BESIDE THE SEASIDE
Grade - Medium

DEESIDE DAWDLE

A - B In Chester centre (see map on page 12) find the canal towpath to Tower Wharf and use the footbridge by the undercover mooring area to access steps onto the road. Head across the road onto Catherine Street. At the end head S/O into the small park area and bear R to pick up the long straight path alongside the River Dee (river on your L). Stay on this excellent, wide tarmac path for about 6 miles, all the way to the railway bridge at Hawarden,

B - A Here head R up the ramp, past Hawarden station, following signs for Chester and Deeside Industrial Park. After 2 miles on superb railpath pass the Millennium Milepost marked Chester, 4 miles (the entrance for 'Once Beside the Seaside' riders). Simply continue for about 3.25 miles then look out for the Millennium Milepost on the bridge over the Shropshire Union Canal. Head dow the ramp and L to retrace the canal towpath back to the city centre and the start.

DEESIDE DAWDLE
Grade - Easy

C-D In Capenhurst pass the church on your L then turn R onto Rectory Lane. Continue along Ledsham Lane to the A550. At the A550 head S/0 using pavement cycle lanes. Turn L onto Badgers Rake Lane. Very shortly NCN Route 56 heads off R up a bridleway but you carry straight on to meet the A540. TAKE CARE to turn R and L here, following signs for Burton. In Burton the road swings R and uphill after passing through the village centre. Just here turn L and descend over the railway to fantastic views across the Dee estuary. Follow the road (Denhall Lane) as it bends 90 degrees R to climb to a T-junction. Turn L towards Ness Botanic Gardens. Just before the Wheatsheaf pub turn L into Well Lane. Meet the road in Neston and go L. Go S/0 a mini-roundabout, following Burton Road into Neston. Head S/0 across a roundabout and in Neston bear L by the drinking fountain onto The Cross, becoming Parkgate Road. Follow this road all the way into Parkgate and head along the 'front' with spectacular marsh views.

D-E Head along Parkgate front and turn R just before the Marsh Cat restaurant and immediate L up School Lane. Bear L onto Brookland Road. Past the primary school pick up the Wirral Way, going under the wooden bridge, bending L up the ramp and L onto the trail. On meeting a B road jink R then L to carry on on the Wirral Way. Over a bridge in Neston head S/0 the car park area, under a rail bridge and follow the road ahead. At the T-junction with Mellock Road/Bushell Rd at the end of Station Close go S/0, onto the Wirral Way. After the cutting carry on on the Wirral Way, past the station building. 0.8 miles after the station you come to a brick bridge over the trail. Turn L off the trail (signed NCN route 56) to a road and R, to cross the bridge. At the L-hand bend turn R onto a track. At the end of this track turn L onto Badgers Rake Lane then bear R up Ledsham Hall Lane to the A550. Cross S/0 to pick up Ledsham Lane.

Towpath continues as Animals & Boats route overleaf

E-A

Back in Capenhurst go R at the end of Rectory Lane, and continue to meet the busy and fast A540. Turn L and R by the Yacht Inn. Descend this pretty, wooded lane down the side of Shotwick Dale to the A550. Take care to head S/0 and into quaint Shotwick village. By the church pick up the marsh access track through the bridleway gate and follow it for over half a mile into Wales. It bends round a small group of houses and under the A548. Here pick up Green Lane West and turn L (Drome Road) to bring you to a major roundabout. Carefully use the pavement and push anti-clockwise round the roundabout, over the A550, taking the exit marked for Sealand and Chester (Green Lane East). Very shortly turn L (marked dead end) and signed RAF Sealand. Go past the RAF base. After 0.75 miles you join NCN route 5 through an access point right by the track. You are now on the superbly-surfaced railpath (follow Millennium Milepost sign for Chester). After 3.3 miles descend onto the canal towpath, bearing L to Chester.

Note on scale: Each blue-lined grid square is 1 kilometre (about 0.6 miles) across

ANIMALS & BOATS

From the centre of Chester find the Shropshire Union Canal towpath (see pg 12 for a detailed city centre map). Heading north carefully negotiate the short, steep gradient at Northgate Staircase Locks to immediately bend R past the broad expanse of Tower Wharf before using the small footbridge to pick up the towpath on the eastern side of the canal and head away from the centre. It's then simply a matter of following the canal for around 8 miles to its end at Ellesmere Port Boat Museum.

B - A

Retrace the canal until passing under bridge 137. Exit at the next concrete bridge (136), going up the access ramp, over the old bridge and R at the road (Stoak village L here). Over the M56 continue into the tiny village of Picton.

Just coming out of Picton turn R onto Ash Hey Lane. At the next T-junction turn R, signed Hoole Bank, Upton & Worthing. Follow Fox Covert Lane over the M53 to meet a T-junction and go L, signed Upton. In Upton Heath turn L at the end of Acres Lane and very shortly R onto Oakfield Drive (NCN route 56). Turn R at the end of Oakfield Drive, marked as a dead end.

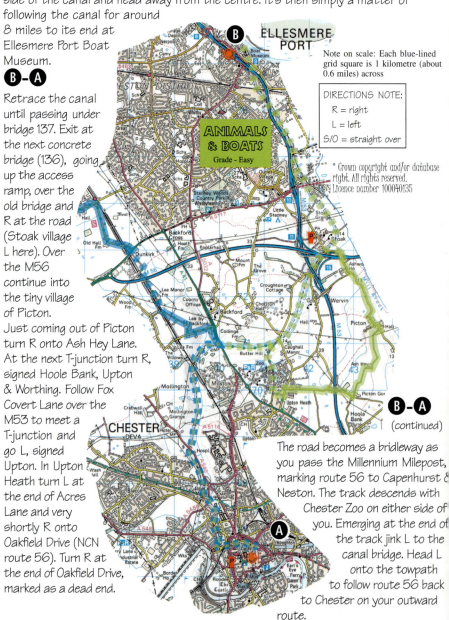

Note on scale: Each blue-lined grid square is 1 kilometre (about 0.6 miles) across

DIRECTIONS NOTE:
R = right
L = left
S/O = straight over

* Crown copyright and/or database right. All rights reserved. Licence number 100040135

B - A

(continued)

The road becomes a bridleway as you pass the Millennium Milepost, marking route 56 to Capenhurst & Neston. The track descends with Chester Zoo on either side of you. Emerging at the end of the track jink L to the canal bridge. Head L onto the towpath to follow route 56 back to Chester on your outward route.

Delamere to Frodsham

Route Info

Forest To River (Medium)
17 miles / 27km
Off - road 5.5 miles / 9km
Height Ascended 216m / 708ft
Suggested Start Delamere station
Route Advice Plenty of reasonable quality off-road riding makes this a ride suitable for older children. There are good wide cinder tracks through Delamere Forest and alongside the Weaver Navigation. Past Dutton Lock the surface is grassy and a bit bumpy but should be fine outside winter. Otherwise you're generally on quiet roads with just a couple of busier, faster sections where care is needed.
Nearest Train Station You can start the route at Delamere station.
Parking Pay & display at Linmere Lodge and opposite Hatch Mere lake (toilets also at both).
Food & Drink Cafes at Delamere Station and Linmere Lodge forest visitor centre. Village shop and pub in Norley. Maypole Inn (see Chapter 1) and others at Acton Bridge.Kingsley has two pubs (Horsehoe Inn and Red Bull) and a mini-Coop store. Carriers Inn at Hatchmere.

Living Marshes (Easy)
11.5 miles / 18.5km
Off - road 8 miles / 13km
Height Ascended 69m / 225ft
Suggested Start Elton station
Route Advice Quiet broad tracks through an unusual landscape. Watch out for agricultural traffic though, especially in late summer when haymaking is taking place.
Nearest Train Station Elton
Parking Elton
Food & Drink The Duke of Wellington pub is at Ince. A rich choice of cafes, pubs and restaurants awaits you in attractive Frodsham.

Forest To Frodsham (Medium)
25.5 miles / 41km
Off - road 7 miles / 11km
Height Ascended 452m / 1483ft
Suggested Start Delamere station
Route Advice Up to Dutton Lock you follow the same mix of good tracks and roads as in the *Forest to River* ride. The good tracks continue as you follow NCN route 56 to Aston before a major road section into Frodsham which requires some care. Out of Frodsham another brief main road section leads to a long but steady climb over the sandstone hills of north Cheshire to finish off using the tracks of Delamere Forest.
Nearest Train Stations You can start the route at Delamere station and there is a station at Frodsham.
Parking Pay & display at Linmere Lodge.
Food & Drink Cafes at Delamere station and at Linmere Lodge forest centre. Pub and village store in Norley. Maypole Inn (see Chapter 1) and others in Acton Bridge. Pubs, restaurants and take aways await you in attractive Frodsham.

Overton Hill Challenge (Difficult)
25 miles / 40km
Off - road 7 miles / 11km
Height Ascended 478m / 1569ft
Suggested Start Delamere station
Route Advice The same route as *Forest to Frodsham* until you reach Frodsham. From here you take a very, very steep climb past Overton Hill, worth a break and a quick walk to see the incredible views over the Mersey estuary. Easier pedalling on country roads with moderate hills awaits you between here and the tracks of Delamere.
Nearest Train Stations You can start the route at Delamere station and there is a station at Frodsham.
Parking Pay & Display, Linmere Lodge
Food & Drink As *Forest to Frodsham*.

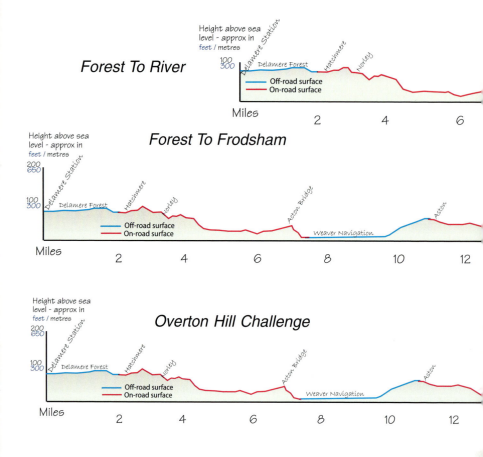

Forest To River

Height above sea level - approx in feet / metres

100 / 300

Delamere Station
Delamere Forest
Hatchmere
Horley

Off-road surface
On-road surface

Miles
2   4   6

Forest To Frodsham

Height above sea level - approx in feet / metres

200 / 650
100 / 300

Delamere Station
Delamere Forest
Hatchmere
Horley
Acton Bridge
Weaver Navigation
Acton

Off-road surface
On-road surface

Miles
2   4   6   8   10   12

Overton Hill Challenge

Height above sea level - approx in feet / metres

200 / 650
100 / 300

Delamere Station
Delamere Forest
Hatchmere
Horley
Acton Bridge
Weaver Navigation
Acton

Off-road surface
On-road surface

Miles
2   4   6   8   10   12

Living Marshes

Height above sea level - approx in feet / metres

100 / 300

Off-road surface
On-road surface

Elton
Ince
Frodsham marshes
Frodsham
Frodsham marshes
Ince
Elton

Miles
2   4   6   8   10

140

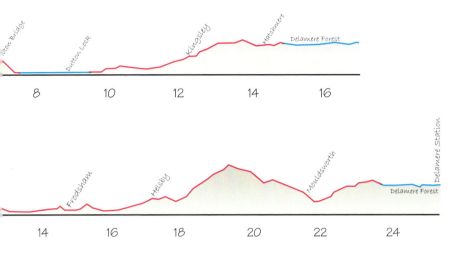

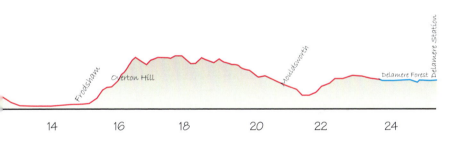

Cross this elegant bridge on the Forest to Frodsham & Overton Hill
Challenge rides

FOREST TO FRODSHAM (A)-(B)

Follow directions **A** to **D** in the Forest to River ride and at Dutton Lock head straight on to cross a lovely white bridge. Bear R over the bridge along the broad fieldside track. Follow NCN 5 signs to split R onto a short section of grassy bridleway before rejoining the main track. At Dutton Lodge Farm turn L, signed Lodge Lane. Descend a short cobbled section and through the gate ascend under a rail bridge and continue climbing on the track until the T-junction with a minor road to go R. At the next T-junction turn L, signed NCN route 5. Pass Aston's church and school and follow this road for around 1 mile to the A56 and go L (CAUTION - BUSY & FAST). Follow the A56 for just over a mile until crossing the second bridge over the Weaver you turn R onto The Quay (leading to Quayside). Very shortly take the first R onto the path marked as The Quay and follow it alongside the River Weaver to pass under the impressive railway viaduct. Through a gate pass the small housing estate and go L at the next T-junction. Meet an estate road and go R onto Waterside Drive to then pass a school on the R. Simply follow the road all the way to Frodsham High St by which time it has become Ship St. Go R here towards Frodsham centre.

Note on scale: Each blue-lined grid square is 1 kilometre (about 0.6 miles) across

B-**C** Follow the A56 down Frodsham Main St and under the railway to go first R onto Dig Lane and go R at the next T-junction. Follow this quiet road and pass under the railway twice to meet the A56 at the end of Godscroft Lane. R onto the A56 cycle lanes and in Helsby turn L up Old Chester Rd and L at the first crossroads up Bates Lane. L onto Tarvin Rd and first R onto the Ridgeway. Follow the long climb to a T-junction and L. Go S/O at the next crossroads onto New Pale Rd.

C-**A** This road has great views and takes you through Manley Common to a crossroads where you go S/O onto Tarvin Road and into Mouldsworth. Past the Goshawk pub and train station turn L onto Delamere Lane, signed Delamere Forest. Take the first R onto Old Lane, signed for Kelsall. Turn R at the next unmarked T-junction and in 0.6 miles turn L onto Forest Farm Road and follow to Eddisbury Fruit Farm. Don't bend R onto Yeld Lane but carry on, on the track signed to Linmere. Simply follow this main track east for around a mile to come back to Linmere Lodge (to get back to Delamere Station just keep going on the main track past Linmere Lodge).

The cafe at Delamere Station is a popular haunt of cyclists

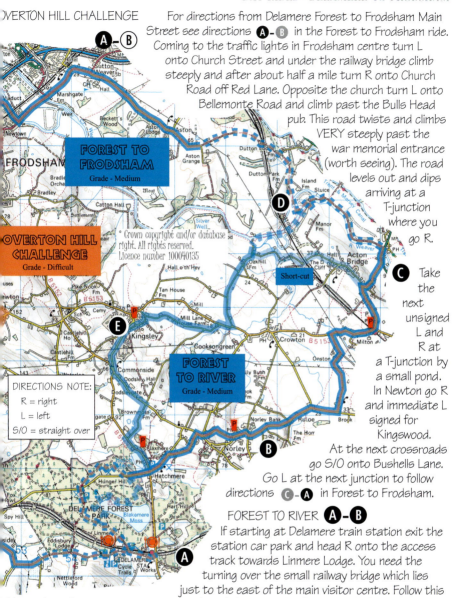

OVERTON HILL CHALLENGE

For directions from Delamere Forest to Frodsham Main Street see directions **A**-**B** in the Forest to Frodsham ride. Coming to the traffic lights in Frodsham centre turn L onto Church Street and under the railway bridge climb steeply and after about half a mile turn R onto Church Road off Red Lane. Opposite the church turn L onto Bellemonte Road and climb past the Bulls Head pub. This road twists and climbs VERY steeply past the war memorial entrance (worth seeing). The road levels out and dips arriving at a T-junction where you go R.

FOREST TO FRODSHAM
Grade - Medium

OVERTON HILL CHALLENGE
Grade - Difficult

© Crown copyright and/or database right. All rights reserved. Licence number 100040135

Short-cut

FOREST TO RIVER
Grade - Medium

DIRECTIONS NOTE:
R = right
L = left
S/O = straight over

C Take the next unsigned L and R at a T-junction by a small pond. In Newton go R and immediate L signed for Kingswood. At the next crossroads go S/O onto Bushells Lane. Go L at the next junction to follow directions **C**-**A** in Forest to Frodsham.

FOREST TO RIVER **A**-**B**

If starting at Delamere train station exit the station car park and head R onto the access track towards Linmere Lodge. You need the turning over the small railway bridge which lies just to the east of the main visitor centre. Follow this wide track until you come to a crossroads with large wooden fingerposts where you go R, following signs for the Hunger Hill biking trail. Follow this track to pass through the Barnsbridge Gate parking area and head straight across the road onto the main forest track to bear R at the first split at marker post 31. Ignore any minor turnings following the track all the way to meet the road again and turn L onto it (TAKE CARE - can be busy and fast) to head into Hatchmere. At the crossroads at the end of Ashton Rd go S/O onto School Lane. The road bends R to become Post Office Lane. Follow this road to a T-junction, going R for Cuddington and Oakmere. In Norley centre turn L down Maddocks Hill. Head L and pass the Tigers Head pub, continuing on Bag Lane out of Norley. Cont. overleaf.

FOREST TO RIVER - *continued from previous page*   **B - C**

1.4 miles out of Norley go L turn onto Onston Lane. R onto the B5153 (Station Rd) and continue past Acton Bridge rail station then turn L onto Hilltop Road. Follow onto Acton Lane and descend to the A49.
(Note: To avoid the riverside section and to shortcut to Kingsley on road, turn L before descending to the A49 and follow Cliff Road through Acton Bridge. Join Cliff Lane and pass under a rail bridge. At the end of Cliff Lane go L to pick up the directions where they are marked* further on in the ride). Go L onto the A49 (WITH CARE) and just across the bridge over the Weaver turn L to the river and head R onto the wide tarmac waterside path with the river on your L.
(Also note underpass option here)

FROM FOREST TO RIVER
Grade - Medium

* Crown copyright and/or database right. All rights reserved. Licence number 100040135

DIRECTIONS NOTE:
R = right
L = left
S/O = straight over

C - D Follow the Weaver for about a mile when it curves L to cross over a minor branch of the river, following the main navigation on your L to come to the impressive Dutton Locks. Cross over the lock gates themselves. NB: If riding the longer Forest to Frodsham option do not cross over the lock gates but carry straight on past Dutton Locks to cross over a beautiful white bridge.

D - E Over Dutton Locks bear R onto the earth/grass track with the Weaver on your R. Through a bridleway gate carry on, on the riverside path to pass under the viaduct. At the end of the grassy field path go through another bridleway gate to pass down a narrow path away from the river and across a small bridge by a caravan park on the right. Bear L, ignoring Cliff Lane on the L, to climb on the road.* At the next split by Oakhill Farm stay R and keep on this road, ignoring Ainsworth Lane on the L. Pass Ball Lane to carry on to a T-junction at the end of Crewood Common Rd and turn R. Take the first L turn onto Roddy Lane. Ignore a minor L and carry on, on Roddy Lane to a T-junction in Kingsley. Turn L onto The Hurst to pass a lovely Methodist church. Turn L onto Top Rd (village services down to the R).

E - A Turn L onto Norley Rd at the crossroads, signed Norley and Cuddington. At the next crossroads turn R onto Forest Lane. L at the next T-junction and shortly pass Hatch Mere lake and the Carriers Inn on the R. Take the next R onto Ashton Rd. In 0.3 miles turn L onto the forest track rejoining the Hunger Hill cycle trail through the forest, following the trackside blue & white topped posts. Follow the cinder and stone track to come to a great view over Blakemere Moss at a T-junction by post 25 and go R. At the next crossroads go S/O signed Linmere Parking Area/Cycle Trails/Delamere Way. Go R at the next fork and L at the next crossroads. On crossing the small bridge over the railway turn R to head back to Linmere parking area or L to head back to the railway station.

A – B Turn R as if emerging from Ince & Elton railway station and follow Station Road all the way into Ince. At the Duke of Wellington pub turn R onto Marsh Lane. Follow Marsh Lane as it bends R and out of Ince the land flattens out as you approach the marshes. Ignore the L split up to Holme Farm, staying on the tarmac surface. At the next split ignore the gravel track to your L. The tarmac turns to earth surface and you cross the tarmac access road into the works. Pass the large chemical works on your R and at the next split carry S/O, ignoring the R which goes via Helsby Marsh into Helsby.

B – C After 0.8 miles head L off the long straight track up a steep incline and bend R to follow this poorer quality track. After around 1.5 miles the track becomes tarmac after Lordship Lane has joined from the R. Pass over the M56 motorway and bend L to follow Marsh Lane to meet the A56 in Frodsham. Take care to turn L onto the A56 and follow it into Frodsham's attractive centre.

C – A Retrace your tracks from Frodsham centre down the A56 and turn R back onto Marsh Lane. Don't recross the M56 but instead turn L onto what appears to be a track by Marsh Green Farm. This shortly turns into a tarmac lane running parallel to the M56 motorway. Follow the lane as it bends R back over the motorway to come to a junction of tracks on the edge of the marshes.

C – A *Cont*
You have three options; take the middle one which leads down a long straight. After about two thirds of a mile pass the track you took earlier up to your R (Cross Lane). Continue on, simply retracing your outward route. Pass the L turn to Helsby and the large chemical works to head back up on Marsh Lane into Ince. L after the Duke of Wellington pub will get you back to Elton.

DIRECTIONS NOTE:

R = right

L = left

S/O = straight over

Note on scale: Each blue-lined grid square is 1 kilometre (about 0.6 miles) across

LIVING MARSHES
Grade - Easy

* Crown copyright and/or database right. All rights reserved. Licence number 100040135

145

Along the Way

Forest to Frodsham

See chapter 1 for details of the visitor centre in Delamere Forest, Norley, Acton Bridge and Mouldsworth Motor Museum.

Dutton Locks, on the Weaver, were built in 1874, the larger lock being an impressive 220 feet long. There is a panoramic view of Dutton railway viaduct.

Frodsham is a busy little town with a wide, flower bedecked main street and a good shopping area. Interesting features include a listed telephone kiosk cum letterbox.

Eddisbury Fruit Farm has a farmshop, open daily, and a farmers' market on the 3rd Saturday of every month.

Overton Hill Challenge

As Forest to Frodsham but with the chance to visit **Overton Hill**, which boasts one of the most spectacularly located war memorials anywhere, sited to give you incredible views over the Mersey to Liverpool. Look out for the gates on the right as you climb steeply out of Frodsham after turning onto Bellemonte Road.

Forest to River

The **Dutton railway viaduct**, an impressive sight with its 22 arches, was built in the 1830s for the Grand Junction Railway and today carries the main West Coast line.

Kingsley is a sizeable village with a shop and post office.

The Carriers Inn at **Hatchmere** has a lovely lakeside location.

Living Marshes

An unusual landscape whose flatness allows you great views of Helsby and Overton Hills to the south plus the opportunity to see such unusual birdlife as peregrine falcons and the thousands of waders that arrive in early April.

Across Frodsham marshes with Helsby Hill in the background

North of Northwich

Route Info

North Of Northwich (Medium)
16 miles / 26km
Off - road 4.5 miles / 7 km
Height Ascended 161m / 530ft
Suggested Start Anderton Boat Lift car park area
Route Advice Excellent quality off-road track through Northwich Country Park and a road closed to motor traffic take you onto roads towards Comberbach and Great Budworth. The bridleway track past Arley Hall is fine but does have a field section. You are then on more minor roads through Antrobus before using the traffic-free tracks of your outward route through Northwich Country Park.
Nearest Train Station Northwich railway station is about two miles from the Anderton boat lift.
Parking There are pay & display car parks near the Anderton Boat Lift and at Marbury Country Park but note the closing times.
Food & Drink There is a cafe at the Anderton Boat Lift. Comberbach has two pubs and there is a pub in Great Budworth, but see Chapter 2 for details of the cafe at Great Budworth Real Dairy Ice Cream. Arley Hall has a cafe. The Antrobus Arms has food at lunchtimes and in the evenings and all day Sunday.

Great Budworth

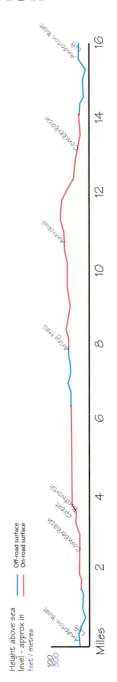

147

* Crown copyright and/or database right. All rights reserved. Licence number 100040135

Note on scale: Each blue-lined grid square is 1 kilometre (about 0.6 miles) across

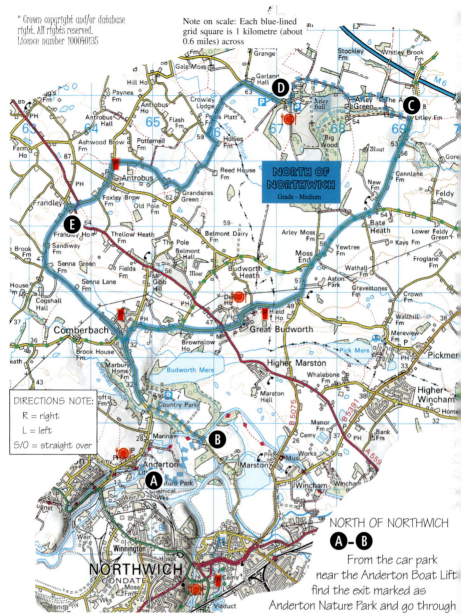

NORTH OF NORTHWICH
Grade - Medium

DIRECTIONS NOTE:
R = right
L = left
S/O = straight over

NORTH OF NORTHWICH

A - B

From the car park near the Anderton Boat Lift find the exit marked as Anderton Nature Park and go through the ornamental 'dragonfly' gate. Immediately the track splits and you bear L, signed Uplands Woodland, Haydn's Pool & Marbury Country Park (R is actually no access for cycles). Follow the main track, ignoring any minor tracks, to then cross a small grass strip to a fingerpost. This points you ahead onto a good track signed for Uplands Woodland, Dairy House Meadows and Marbury Country Park, to immediately pass the sculpture sign for Uplands Woodland. Descend and climb over the bridge at Lesley's Leap. Follow the track to meet the tarmacked Marbury Lane and go L onto it. Cross the Trent and Mersey Canal

B-C   Follow Marbury Lane to pass the car park at Marbury Country Park and go R at the T-junction. Follow the road into Comberbach and just past the Spinner & Bergamot pub turn R, signed Great Budworth. Follow this road to the A559 and go S/O into Great Budworth. Follow the road to a T-junction and go L onto Budworth Road, signed High Legh and Knutsford. At the hamlet of Bate Heath turn L onto Cann Lane, signed for High Legh. Follow this road for just under a mile.

C-D   Just before Litley Farm turn L onto a road marked as a private road but also signed to Arley Hall & Gardens and as a public bridleway. There is also a rhyming fingerpost (see Along the Way - Arley Hall). At Mill House turn R onto the signed bridleway. Follow the track and bear L before the five-bar gate to continue on the bridleway track. Bear R and L following the sign marked as 'Via Back Lane to Arley' to go through a gate into a field, where you head across it towards the copse of trees and pick up a narrow dirt path along the edge of the trees. At the end of the field go through the gate onto a tarmac road and go R, following the bridleway signs. Ignore the R up to Stockley Farm and at the next crossroads head S/O onto public road, to the car park and entrance for Arley Hall on the L.

D-E   After a visit to Arley Hall (see Along the Way) go back to the crossroads and L to another crossroads and L again. Pass Crowley Lodge and at the T-junction at the end of Lodge Lane go L onto Hollins Lane. Turn R at Grandsires Green Farm onto Keepers Lane. Follow this road, ignoring any R turns, to a T-junction and go L to come into Antrobus. At the next T-junction go L then immediate R signed Frandley, opposite the village shop. Continue on School Lane to meet the A559. WITH CARE go L and immediate R, signed Frandley. (Note - the Antrobus Arms is just off the route here up to the R along the A559).

E-A   In Frandley bear L following signs for Comberbach and Little Leigh. Pass the R turn of Scotch Hall Lane and come to a split to bear L signed Comberbach and Northwich. Follow this lane for over a mile, staying on Senna Lane to pass Cogshall Lane on the R in Comberbach, and meet a T-junction to go R onto Marbury Road. Turn L, signed Marbury Country Park and as a no through road. It's now just a case of following your outward route along Marbury Lane and woodland and field tracks to the car park near the Anderton Boat Lift

Look out for the unique rhyming bridleway signs around Arley Hall

Along the Way

North of Northwich

There are details of the Anderton Boat Lift, Comberbach and Great Budworth in Chapter 2.

The **Anderton Nature Park** and **Marbury Country Park** are large areas of rolling land criss-crossed by a network of signed paths and are big enough to swallow up the large number of visitors. Anderton Nature Park is recovered industrial land and Marbury Country Park, where there are toilets, is the estate land of the former Marbury Hall and fronts on to Budworth Mere.

Arley Hall and Gardens are open to the public between April and October and apart from the house and gardens offer a cafe, a working farm and an adventure playground. Telephone 01565 777353 or see www.arleyhallandgardens.com.

There are large **wooden fingerposts** here and there around the paths on Arley with rhyming messages on them, apparently the work of Rowland Egerton Warburton, who built the present hall.

Antrobus and **Frandley** are picturesque.

Quiet lanes on the northern part of the ride

Multi-day Rides

The following suggested rides are brief outlines for routes of between 49 and 62 miles - good distances for covering over two or three days at a leisurely pace. Whilst they are ideal for weekend trips you'll find that many of the minor roads they use are even quieter during mid-week and outside of car commuting times (i.e. very generally between 9.30am and 3pm) when you have many of the roads pretty much to yourself.

The majority of each ride uses sections of other signed routes, most of which are linear (see pages 4-7 in the introduction for more explanation of the individual signed routes). By linking these together you have signed leisure routes which let you explore both the main tourist attractions and the equally interesting rural backwaters of this lovely county. Although you should be able to navigate from these maps and by using the cycle signs along the way, it's much safer to get hold of the appropriate OS maps which are listed in the Route Info section for each ride and use these as backup. Each ride also gives a summary of which numbered routes you will need to follow and between which locations and a handy statistical summary for those who like to count miles covered and feet climbed.

KEY TO MULTI-DAY RIDE MAPS

Line of route (green overlay)

Motorway

'A' roads

'B' roads

Minor roads

Chester

City

Norley

Town or village

Off-road tracks

Railway line and station

Rivers and canals

These routes are ideal for light, fast touring with minimal luggage

North of Chester

Route Info

Highlights Chester's historic centre, Parkgate's seafront, Frodsham Marshes and Frodsham's main street, Dutton Locks on the Weaver Navigation and the Roman bridges at Hockenhull Platts between the pretty villages of Tarvin and Christleton.
Route Stats 61 miles / 98km   Off - road 17.5 miles / 28 km
Height Ascended 680m / 2231ft
Possible Overnight Stays
Two day route Chester-Frodsham (35 miles), Frodsham-Chester (26 miles)
Three day route Chester-Parkgate (15 miles), Parkgate-Frodsham (20 miles), Frodsham-Chester (26 miles)
Maps Ordnance Survey Landranger 117 Chester and Wrexham (a tiny part of the route just spills over onto Landranger 118 Stoke-on-Trent & Macclesfield)

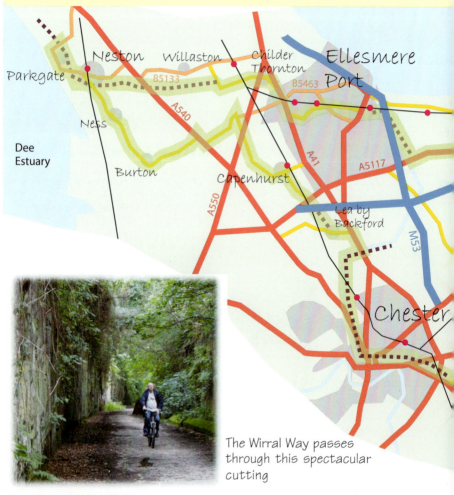

The Wirral Way passes through this spectacular cutting

SIGNED ROUTES FOLLOWED - For a full explanation of routes and route signs in Cheshire see pages 4 to 7

Chester to A5117 Ellesmere Port   Head out of Chester centre on the canal towpath, exiting at the A41 before heading on tracks then roads through the Wirral to the coast at Parkgate. The Wirral Way takes you to Ellesmere Port before heading south on the towpath to the A5117.

A5117 to Acton Bridge NCN 5. Drop off the A5117 cycle lane to cross Frodsham marshes on wide bridleway tracks. Through Frodsham a brief section of busy A-road leads to a lovely track section coming alongside the River Weaver all the way to Acton Bridge.

Acton Bridge to near Mouldsworth Follow the Cheshire Cycleway on mainly minor roads from Acton Bridge to just before Mouldsworth.

Near Mouldsworth to South of Kelsall Follow signs taking you towards route 71 on minor roads
South of Kelsall to Christleton Use route 71 on minor roads to Tarvin then cross Hockenhull Platts on a beautiful bridleway section before more minor roads to Christleton

Christleton to Chester An easy and attractive towpath ride back to Chester centre on route 70/71

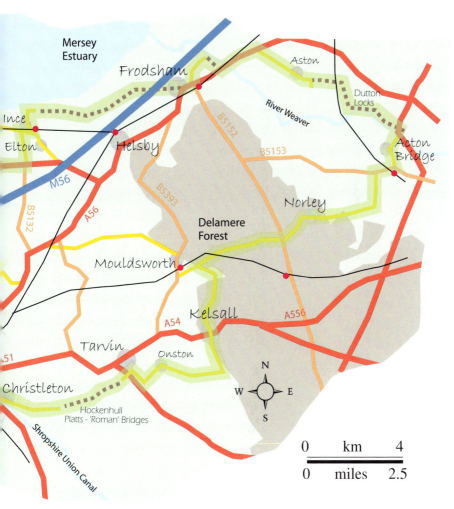

Route Info

Highlights Beautiful mid-Cheshire villages of Tarporley and Tarvin, South Peckforton Hills, Cholmondeley Castle Gardens, quiet lanes linking lovely Marbury, Wrenbury and Audlem, Hack Green Nuclear Bunker, Bunbury

Route Stats 49 miles / 79km

Off - road 0 miles (3 day option with Malpas and Nantwich is 60 miles - 0 miles off-road)

Height Ascended 552m / 1812ft

Possible Overnight Stays

Two day route Tarporley-Audlem (28 miles), Audlem-Tarporley (21 miles)

Three day route Tarporley-Malpas (19 miles), Malpas-Nantwich (25 miles), Nantwich-Tarporley (16 miles)

Maps Ordnance Survey Landranger 117 Chester and Wrexham & 118 Stoke-on-Trent & Macclesfield

The Peckfortons & the South

SIGNED ROUTES FOLLOWED

Tarporley to Huxley Signed as the link route between routes 70 and 71 and then as route 70

Huxley to Bickley Moss (A49) Head across the glorious scenery of the southern Peckfortons and south of Cholmondeley Castle cross the A49. Parts of this section also use route 70 (Cheshire Cycleway)

Bickley Moss (A49) to Audlem Just follow Cheshire Cycleway signs on quiet roads all the way to lovely Audlem.

Audlem to Ravensmoor Follow route 75 signs to Ravensmoor where you meet route 74 from Wrenbury and Crewe

Ravensmoor to Tarporley Follow signs taking you towards route 70 at Beeston and from there use route 70 to rejoin outward route back to Tarporley

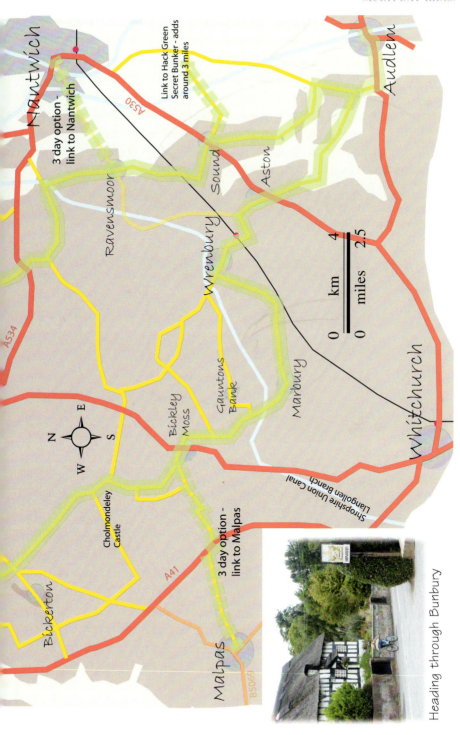

Nantwich

3 day option - link to Nantwich

Link to Hack Green Secret Bunker - adds around 3 miles

A530

Ravensmoor

Wrenbury

Sound

Aston

Audlem

km
0   4

miles
0   2.5

Marbury

Whitchurch

Gauntons Bank

Bickley Moss

N
E
S
W

Shropshire Union Canal
Llangollen Branch

A534

Cholmondeley Castle

3 day option - link to Malpas

A41

Bickerton

Malpas

B5069

Heading through Bunbury

155

The South East

Route Info

Highlights

Historic Nantwich's centre, quiet lanes and villages between Nantwich and Winsford, River Dane scenery and beautiful bridleway tracks approaching pretty Swettenham, Astbury church, villages of the south-east (Barthomley, Hassall Green and Wybunbury)

Route Stats

53 miles / 85km
Off-road 5 miles / 8km

Height Ascended
617m / 2026ft

Possible Overnight Stays

Two day route
Nantwich-Congleton (31 miles), Congleton-Nantwich (22 miles)

Three day route
Nantwich-Middlewich (15 miles), Middlewich-Hassall Green (22 miles), Hassall Green-Nantwich (16 miles)

Maps Ordnance Survey Landranger 118 Stoke-on-Trent & Macclesfield

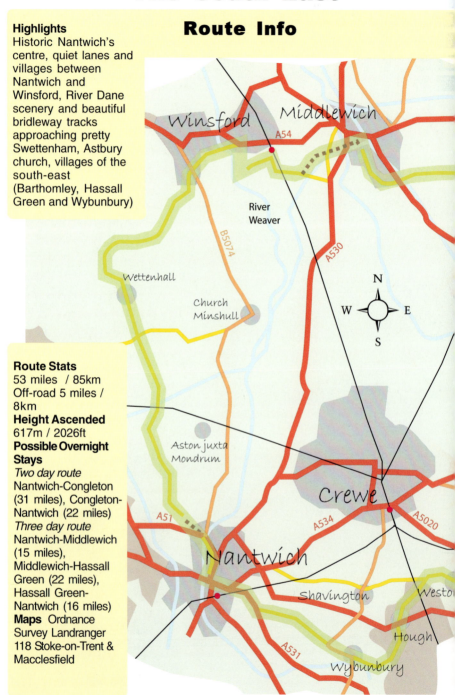

SIGNED ROUTES FOLLOWED

Nantwich to Winsford Follow quiet roads on route 75 through tiny villages and hamlets
Winsford to Middlewich This section uses a mixture of tracks (including canal towpath on your approach to Middlewich) and minor roads, tracing NCN route 55
Middlewich to north of Newsbank A lovely section through mid-Cheshire's green scenery along route 71. Mainly minor roads with great tracks approaching Swettenham
North of Newsbank to Nantwich NCN 55 takes you into Congleton from where you pick up the link route to the Cheshire Cycleway, route 70. After a string of lovely villages including Hassall Green, Barthomley and Weston come to Wybunbury and then use the B5071 to pick up the minor road to Butt Green. From here use main roads into Nantwich.

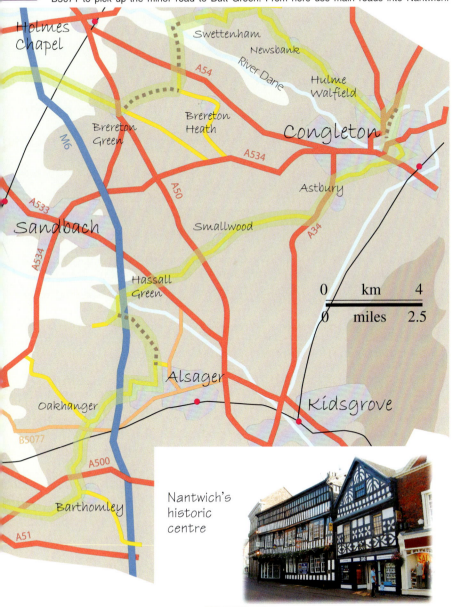

Nantwich's historic centre

Ridge to Sea
Teggs Nose to Parkgate

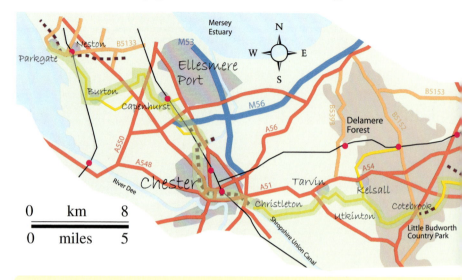

Route Info

Highlights Teggs Nose Country Park gritstone scenery, Gawsworth Hall, Swettenham and Davenport Hall bridleway, the 'Roman' bridges at Hockenhull Platts between the pretty villages of Tarvin and Christleton, Chester's historic centre, Parkgate seafront

Route Stats
62 miles / 100km   Off - road 4.5 miles / 7 km

Height Ascended 728m / 2390ft - though note you also descend around 1075m / 3530ft partly due to the long downhill run away from Teggs Nose Country Park!

Possible Overnight Stays
Two day route Teggs Nose-Cotebrook (32 miles), Cotebrook-Parkgate (30 miles)
Note: Tarporley is just off the route near Cotebrook and would be a good overnight stop
Three day route Teggs Nose-Middlewich (21 miles), Middlewich-Tarvin (18.5 miles), Tarvin-Parkgate (22.5 miles)

Maps Ordnance Survey Landranger 117 Chester and Wrexham & 118 Stoke-on-Trent & Macclesfield

Signed Route

Simply follow route 71 signs all the way from Teggs Nose Country Park to Parkgate as this is Regional Route 71 in its entirety. The route also doubles up with some other sections of route - for example it uses the Cheshire Cycleway between Sutton Lane Ends and north of Congleton. Despite the presence of other route signs you should always be able to follow route 71 signs however.

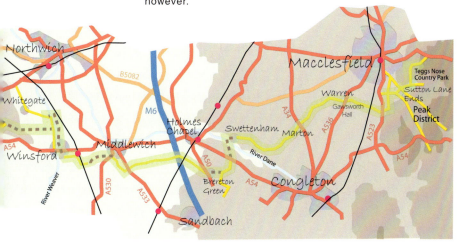

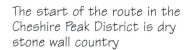

The start of the route in the Cheshire Peak District is dry stone wall country

INDEX

MAIN SETTLEMENTS AND FEATURES

160